Gooseberry Patch co. ®

AUTUMN
In the Country

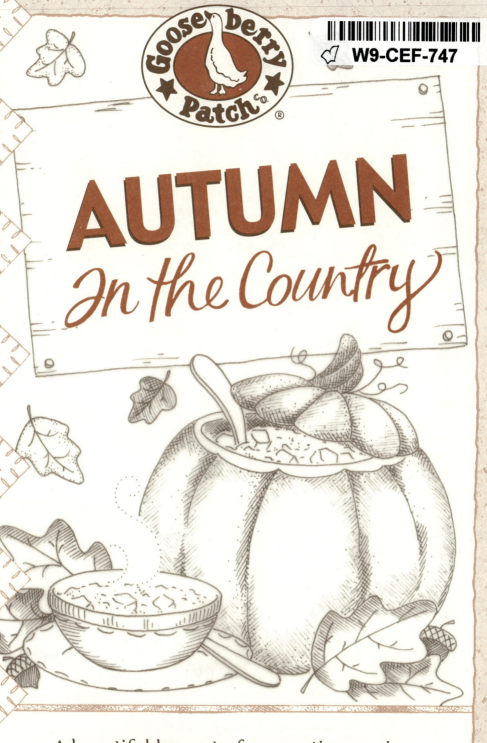

A bountiful harvest of scrumptious recipes,
plus fall fun in the country with family & friends.

A Country Store In Your Mailbox®

Gooseberry Patch
600 London Road
P.O. Box 190
Delaware, OH 43015

www.gooseberrypatch.com
1·800·854·6673

Copyright 2007, Gooseberry Patch 978-1-933494-22-7
First Printing, May, 2007

Do you have a tried & true recipe...

tip, craft or memory that you'd like to see featured in a **Gooseberry
Patch** book? Visit our website at **www.gooseberrypatch.com**, register
and follow the easy steps to submit your favorite family recipe.
Or send them to us at:

Gooseberry Patch
Attn: Book Dept.
P.O. Box 190
Delaware, OH 43015

Don't forget to include the number of servings your recipe makes,
plus your name, address, phone number and e-mail address.
If we select your recipe, your name will appear right along
with it...and you'll receive a **FREE** copy of the book!

CONTENTS

DEDICATION

To everyone who loves brisk autumn days,
the spicy sweetness of pumpkin pie and
Thanksgiving at Grandma's house.

APPRECIATION

For our families & friends...a bushel basket
of thanks for sharing your yummiest recipes.

A Cozy Country
BRUNCH

Caramel French Toast

Erin Diaz
Hammonton, NJ

So warm & cozy on a chilly fall morning.

1-1/2 c. brown sugar, packed
1 c. butter, divided
1/4 c. plus 2 T. light corn syrup
10 thick slices French bread
4 eggs, beaten

2-1/2 c. half-and-half or milk
1 T. vanilla extract
1/4 t. salt
3 T. sugar
1-1/2 t. cinnamon

Combine brown sugar, 3/4 cup butter and corn syrup in a medium saucepan. Cook over medium heat, stirring constantly, for 5 minutes or until bubbly. Pour mixture into a lightly greased 13"x9" baking pan; arrange bread in pan and set aside. Combine eggs, half-and-half or milk, vanilla and salt; stir well. Gradually pour egg mixture over bread. Cover and chill at least 7 to 8 hours. Combine sugar and cinnamon; sprinkle evenly over bread. Melt remaining butter; drizzle over bread. Bake, uncovered, at 350 degrees for 45 to 50 minutes, until golden and bubbly. Serve immediately. Makes 10 servings.

The air is brisk and the leaves are turning...it's autumn!
Spend the weekend at a country cabin...invite family & friends
to a cozy brunch at home. It's a wonderful time for food and fun.

Pumpkin Pancakes

Joyce LaMure
Reno, NV

*Create funny Jack-'O-Lantern faces with chocolate chips
to make the kids giggle!*

2 c. all-purpose flour
2 T. brown sugar, packed
1 T. baking powder
1 t. salt
1 t. cinnamon
1/4 t. nutmeg

1/4 t. ground ginger
1/2 c. canned pumpkin
1-1/2 c. milk
1 egg, lightly beaten
2 T. oil

Combine flour, brown sugar, baking powder, salt and spices in a large bowl; set aside. Combine remaining ingredients in a separate bowl; mix well. Stir pumpkin mixture into flour mixture just until moistened. Pour batter by 1/4 cupfuls onto a lightly greased hot griddle. Cook until bubbles appear on the surface; turn and continue cooking for an additional 2 to 3 minutes, until golden. Makes 16 pancakes.

Put out a country-style welcome! Arrange fallen autumn
leaves around a plain jute doormat and spray carefully
with indoor-outdoor paint in russet, brown or gold.
Remove leaves after paint has dried...how clever!

Easy Lemon-Lime Ham

Claire Bertram
Lexington, KY

*Delicious served warm for brunch or dinner...it makes
scrumptious cold sandwiches too.*

3 to 4-lb. boneless
   fully-cooked ham
12-oz. can lemon-lime soda
1/4 c. honey

1/2 t. dry mustard
1/2 t. ground cloves
1/4 t. cinnamon

Place ham in a slow cooker and add soda. Cover and cook on low
setting for 6 to 8 hours, or on high setting for 3 to 4 hours. About
30 minutes before serving, combine 3 tablespoons drippings from
slow cooker with honey, mustard and spices. Mix well and spread over
ham. Cover and continue cooking on low setting for final 30 minutes.
Remove to a platter; let stand for 15 minutes before slicing. Makes
12 to 16 servings.

Back-to-school time isn't just for kids.
Treat yourself to a craft class like knitting, quilting
or scrapbooking that you've been longing to try...
take a girlfriend along with you!

Sunday Brunch Casserole

Zoe Groff
Lebanon, TN

*Overnight guests will love waking up to this tasty dish.
Just prepare the night before, cover and refrigerate
unbaked…in the morning, pop it in the oven.*

1/2 lb. bacon, crisply cooked,
    crumbled and drippings
    reserved
1/2 c. onion, chopped
1/2 c. green pepper, chopped
1 doz. eggs
1 c. milk

20-oz. pkg. frozen shredded
    hashbrowns, thawed
1 c. shredded Cheddar cheese
1 t. salt or seasoned salt
1/2 t. pepper
1/2 t. dill weed

Heat reserved drippings in a large skillet over medium heat. Add
onion and green pepper; cook until tender and set aside. Whisk
together eggs and milk in a large bowl; stir in bacon, onion mixture
and hashbrowns. Mix in cheese and seasonings. Transfer to a greased
13"x9" baking pan. Bake, uncovered, at 350 degrees for 35 to
45 minutes, or until a knife inserted near the center comes out clean.
Makes 8 to 12 servings.

Pull out Grandma's vintage casserole dishes...
they're just right for baking hearty fall casseroles
and desserts, with a side dish of nostalgia!

Cherry-Almond Scones

Nicole Shira
New Baltimore, MI

Drizzle with white icing for a sweet finish.

2 c. all-purpose flour
1/3 c. sugar
1 T. poppy seed
1 t. baking powder
1/2 t. salt

3/4 c. butter
1/3 c. sour cream
1 egg, beaten
2 t. almond extract
1/2 c. sweetened, dried cherries

Combine first 5 ingredients in a food processor; process until well blended. Add butter; process until mixture resembles coarse crumbs. Set aside. In a bowl, whisk together sour cream, egg and extract; stir into flour mixture. Mix in cherries; pat out to 1/4-inch thickness on a floured surface. Use a 2-inch round cookie cutter to cut out; place on an ungreased baking sheet. Bake at 400 degrees for 10 to 12 minutes. Makes 8 to 10.

Cappuccino Muffins

Sharon Demers
Dolores, CO

These muffins smell heavenly while they're baking.

2 c. all-purpose flour
3/4 c. sugar
2-1/2 t. baking powder
1/2 t. salt
2 T. baking cocoa
1 c. milk

2 T. instant coffee granules
1 egg, beaten
1/2 c. butter, melted
1 t. vanilla extract
3/4 c. mini semi-sweet
   chocolate chips

Combine first 5 ingredients in a large bowl; set aside. Mix together milk, coffee and egg; stir into flour mixture. Stir in butter and vanilla; mix well. Stir in chocolate chips. Spoon batter into paper-lined or greased muffin cups, filling 2/3 full. Bake at 375 degrees for 17 to 20 minutes, until a toothpick tests clean. Cool in pan for 5 minutes; transfer to a wire rack to finish cooling. Makes one dozen.

Old-Timey Drop Doughnuts

Sharon Crider
Junction City, KS

So much better than store-bought doughnuts!

2 eggs
1 c. sugar, divided
1 T. shortening, melted
1 c. milk
1 t. vanilla extract

3-1/2 c. all-purpose flour
2 t. baking powder
1/8 t. salt
1/2 t. cinnamon
oil for deep frying

In a mixing bowl, beat eggs until light; blend in 1/2 cup sugar, shortening, milk and vanilla. Set aside. Combine flour, baking powder and salt in another mixing bowl; stir into egg mixture to make a soft dough. Mix together cinnamon and remaining sugar; set aside. Heat several inches oil to 365 degrees in a deep saucepan. Drop dough into hot oil by teaspoonfuls, a few at a time. Fry until doughnuts turn themselves over and are golden on all sides. Drain on paper towels; roll in cinnamon mixture while still warm. Makes 3 dozen.

Company's coming! Stock the guest room with a basket of sweet-smelling bath treats, a fluffy comforter and a plate of freshly baked cookies...all things that say "We're glad you're here!"

Tracie's Ham & Spinach Quiche

Tracie Daugherty
Kittanning, PA

My family enjoys this easy dish morning, noon or night. Try adding a different cheese or veggie for a change.

1 doz. eggs
1 pt. whipping cream
1/2 t. garlic powder
1/2 t. dried oregano
1/8 t. pepper
1 c. cooked ham, finely diced

10-oz. pkg. frozen spinach,
   cooked and drained
1/3 c. onion, finely diced
8-oz. pkg. shredded Cheddar
   cheese

Beat together eggs and cream, blending well. Add seasonings; mix well. Sprinkle ham, spinach, onion and cheese evenly into a lightly greased 13"x9" baking pan; slowly pour egg mixture over top. Bake at 350 degrees for 45 to 50 minutes, until top is golden and knife inserted into center comes out clean. Cool slightly before cutting into squares. Serves 6 to 8.

The first weekend of fall color, pack a picnic lunch and hop in the car. Take a favorite route or go down that country lane you've always wondered about...who knows where it will lead!

A Cozy Country
BRUNCH

Smoked Gouda Grits

Becky Woods
Ballwin, MO

Serve with scrambled eggs and breakfast sausage...yum!

6 c. chicken broth
2 c. milk
1 t. salt
1/2 t. white pepper
2 c. quick-cooking grits,
   uncooked

1-2/3 c. smoked Gouda cheese,
   shredded
3 T. butter, softened

Bring broth, milk, salt and pepper to a boil in a large saucepan over medium heat. Gradually whisk in grits. Reduce heat; cover and simmer, stirring occasionally, for about 5 minutes until thickened. Add cheese and butter; stir until melted. Serves 6 to 8.

Fried Cornmeal Mush

Pam Vienneau
West Haven, CT

An old-fashioned treat...serve hot with maple syrup.

4 c. cold water, divided
1 t. salt

1 c. cornmeal
3 T. butter, divided

Bring 3 cups water to a boil in a medium saucepan; mix in salt. Mix cornmeal with remaining cold water in a small bowl; stir into boiling water. Stir until thickened. Cover; cook over low heat for 10 minutes. Mix in one tablespoon butter. Spoon into a greased 9"x 5" loaf pan; cover and chill overnight. To serve, unmold loaf pan; cut into 1/2-inch slices. In a skillet over medium heat, fry in remaining butter until golden on both sides. Serves 6 to 8.

Paint names on colorful mini gourds
for whimsical placecards.

Country Morning Coffee Cake

Brenda Huey
Geneva, IN

You'll love this moist coffee cake.

1 c. margarine, softened
2 c. sugar
4 eggs, beaten
2 c. sour cream
4 c. all-purpose flour

2 t. baking soda
2 t. baking powder
1 t. salt
2 t. vanilla extract

Combine margarine, sugar, eggs and sour cream in a large bowl. Stir in remaining ingredients; mix thoroughly. Pour into a greased 15"x10" jelly-roll pan; sprinkle with Cinnamon-Pecan Topping. Bake at 350 degrees for 25 minutes, until a toothpick tests clean. Cut into squares. Serves 18 to 20.

Cinnamon-Pecan Topping:

2/3 c. brown sugar, packed
1/2 c. sugar

2 t. cinnamon
1/2 c. chopped pecans

Use a fork to mix all ingredients together.

Roll up homespun napkins, tie with ribbon bows and slip
a sprig of bittersweet under the ribbons...simple!

A Cozy Country
BRUNCH

Molasses Buns

Patsy Leaman
Crockett, TX

Sweet and spicy...you'll want more than one!

1/2 c. boiling water
1/2 c. butter, melted
1/2 c. molasses
1/2 c. sugar   ·
2 t. baking soda

1/2 t. ground cloves
1/2 t. cinnamon
1/2 t. nutmeg
3 c. all-purpose flour

Mix together all ingredients except flour; set aside until cool. Stir in flour; let stand for 20 minutes. Roll into balls by tablespoonfuls; place on greased baking sheets. Flatten balls with a spoon; bake at 375 degrees for 20 minutes. Makes about 20 buns.

Grandma's Warm Breakfast Fruit

Virginia Watson
Scranton, PA

Keep this warm for brunch in a mini slow cooker.

3 cooking apples, cored, peeled
    and thickly sliced
1 orange, peeled and sectioned
3/4 c. raisins
1/2 c. dried plums, chopped

3 c. plus 3 T. water, divided
1/2 c. sugar
1/2 t. cinnamon
2 T. cornstarch

Combine fruit and 3 cups water in a saucepan over medium heat. Bring to a boil; reduce heat and simmer for 10 minutes. Stir in sugar and cinnamon. In a small bowl, mix together cornstarch and remaining water; stir into fruit mixture. Bring to a boil, stirring constantly; cook for 2 minutes. Serve warm or cold. Serves 6 to 8.

Autumn...the year's last, loveliest smile.

-William Cullen Bryant

Southern Corned Beef Hash

Tammy Williams
West Carthage, NY

Top each portion with an egg cooked sunny-side up.

1 to 2 T. oil
6 to 8 potatoes, peeled,
   diced and cooked

1 onion, diced
2 12-oz. cans corned beef, diced
salt and pepper to taste

Heat oil in a large skillet over medium heat; add potatoes, onion and corned beef. Cook over low heat for about 10 minutes, until crisp and golden. Add salt and pepper to taste. Serves 4 to 6.

Praline Bacon

Vickie

Crispy bacon with a chili kick!

1 lb. bacon
3 T. brown sugar, packed

1-1/2 t. chili powder
1/4 c. finely chopped pecans

Line 2 baking sheets with aluminum foil; spray with non-stick vegetable spray. Arrange bacon in a single layer on prepared baking sheets. Bake at 425 degrees for 10 minutes; drain. Combine brown sugar and chili powder; sprinkle over bacon. Top with pecans. Bake for an additional 5 to 10 minutes, until bacon is crisp. Drain on paper towels. Serves 6 to 8.

Set out a wooden bowl of walnuts so everyone
can help themselves...don't forget the nutcracker!

Potato-Bacon Breakfast Pie

Marsha Konken
Sterling, CO

Just add cinnamon rolls and fresh fruit for a complete meal.

1 lb. bacon, crisply cooked
   and crumbled
9-inch pie crust
2 c. frozen shredded
   hashbrowns, thawed

1/2 c. shredded Cheddar cheese
4 eggs, beaten
1/4 c. milk

Arrange bacon in pie crust; layer evenly with hashbrowns and cheese. Combine eggs and milk; pour over cheese. Bake at 350 degrees for 40 minutes, until center is set. Let stand for 5 minutes before slicing into wedges. Serves 4 to 6.

Warm Spiced Apricot Punch

Jill Valentine
Jackson, TN

The spicy scent will welcome everyone to breakfast.

2 12-oz. cans apricot nectar
2 c. water
1/4 c. lemon juice

1/4 c. sugar
6 whole cloves
2 4-inch cinnamon sticks

Combine all ingredients in a slow cooker; mix well. Cover and cook on low setting for 2 hours. Strain to remove spices before serving. Serves 6.

Watch for old-fashioned syrup pitchers at tag sales...set out a variety of sweet toppings like flavored syrups and honey for pancakes and waffles.

Corn Waffles

Kerry Mayer
Dunham Springs, LA

Delicious served with sliced honey ham.

1-3/4 c. self-rising flour
1/3 c. sugar
1/2 t. salt
3 eggs, separated

1/2 c. buttermilk
1/3 c. oil
1 c. frozen corn, thawed
Garnish: butter, maple syrup

Combine flour, sugar and salt in a large bowl; make a well in the center. Whisk together egg yolks, buttermilk, oil and corn; add to dry ingredients, stirring just until moistened. Set aside. In a separate bowl, beat egg whites with an electric mixer on high speed until stiff peaks form; fold into batter. Spoon by 1/4 cupfuls onto a greased waffle iron; bake according to manufacturer's directions until golden. Makes ten, 4-inch waffles.

Stir up a super-simple fruit topping for pancakes and waffles. Combine a can of fruit pie filling and 2 tablespoons orange juice in a small bowl. Microwave for 2 to 2-1/2 minutes, stirring twice. Yum!

Snickerdoodle Mini Muffins

Jennifer Le
Salt Lake City, UT

Everyone's favorite cookie in the form of bite-size muffins!

1-1/2 c. all-purpose flour
1 c. quick-cooking oats,
   uncooked
3/4 c. sugar, divided
1 T. baking powder

1 c. milk
1 egg, beaten
1/4 c. margarine, softened
1 t. vanilla extract
1 t. cinnamon

Combine flour, oats, 1/2 cup sugar and baking powder; mix well. In a separate bowl, combine milk, egg, margarine and vanilla; blend well and add to flour mixture. Fill greased mini muffin cups 2/3 full. Mix together cinnamon and remaining sugar; sprinkle over muffins. Bake at 400 degrees for 12 to 14 minutes. Makes 3 dozen.

Brown Sugar Bacon

Kathy Grashoff
Fort Wayne, IN

A tasty side for a hot brunch buffet.

1 lb. sliced Canadian bacon
1/4 c. brown sugar, packed

1/4 c. pineapple juice
1/4 t. dry mustard

Arrange bacon slices in a lightly greased 11"x7" baking pan; set aside. Combine remaining ingredients; pour over bacon. Cover and bake at 325 degrees for 25 to 30 minutes, until heated through. Serves 6 to 8.

Newly picked gourds will stay colorful much longer if they're washed in a mild (10%) bleach solution and air dried.

Sweet Cinnamon Biscuits

Amy Woods
Collinsville, TX

Absolutely delicious with hot coffee...and the aroma while they're baking is sure to bring back childhood memories of home.

2 c. all-purpose flour
1 T. baking powder
1/4 t. baking soda
1 t. salt
1/4 c. oil

3/4 c. buttermilk
1/2 c. butter, softened
3/4 c. sugar
1 t. cinnamon
1/4 t. ground cardamom

Combine first 4 ingredients in a large bowl; mix well. Stir in oil; add buttermilk and stir just until blended. Knead dough on a lightly floured surface until smooth; roll out into a 15"x8" rectangle. Spread butter over dough. Combine sugar and spices; sprinkle over butter. Starting on one long side, roll up jelly-roll style. Pinch seam together. Cut roll into 1-1/2 inch thick slices; arrange cut-side up in a lightly greased 9" round cake pan. Bake at 400 degrees for 15 to 20 minutes, until lightly golden. Makes about 10 biscuits.

Amaretto Coffee Creamer

Marlene Darnell
Newport Beach, CA

Makes a cup of coffee extra special.

3/4 c. powdered non-dairy
    coffee creamer
3/4 c. powdered sugar

1 t. cinnamon
1 t. almond extract

Combine all ingredients in an airtight container; shake well to blend. Store in an airtight container. Makes about 1-1/2 cups.

Listen to fallen leaves crunching underfoot...
rake them up and jump in the pile, if you dare!

Viennese Coffee

Regina Vining
Warwick, RI

Warming after an afternoon of antique shopping with friends.

3 c. strong brewed coffee
3 T. chocolate syrup
1 t. sugar
1/3 c. whipping cream

Optional: 1/3 c. chocolate liqueur
Garnish: whipped topping,
    chocolate shavings

Combine coffee, syrup and sugar in a slow cooker. Cover and cook on low setting for 2 to 2-1/2 hours. Stir in cream and liqueur, if using. Cover and cook on low setting for an additional 30 minutes, or until heated through. Ladle into mugs; garnish with dollops of whipped topping and chocolate shavings. Makes 4 servings.

Buttermint Coffee Creamer

Tiffany Brinkley
Broomfield, CO

For a fun gift, pack in mini jars…wrap some more
mints in circles of tulle and tie onto jars for nibbling.

7-oz. pkg. buttermints, crushed
2 c. powdered non-dairy
    coffee creamer

2 c. chocolate malt powder
1/2 c. chocolate drink mix

Combine all ingredients in a blender. Process at high spend until well blended. Store in an airtight container. Makes about 5 cups.

Pick up some sturdy vintage mugs at
tag sales for serving hot beverages.
They hold the heat well…wonderful
to wrap chilly fingers around!

Salli's Sausage Breakfast Bake

*Salli Villeneuve
Milton, VT*

*Hearty and filling...afterwards, you'll be ready for
a brisk hike in the woods!*

1 lb. ground pork sausage
2 T. all-purpose flour
1-1/2 c. milk
1/2 t. salt
1 t. pepper
20-oz. pkg. frozen shredded
   hashbrowns

4 green onions, chopped
   and divided
1-1/4 c. shredded sharp
   Cheddar cheese, divided

Brown sausage in a skillet over medium heat, about 5 minutes; drain. Sprinkle flour over sausage, stirring to combine; cook for one minute. Slowly add milk; bring to a boil, stirring often, until mixture thickens. Simmer for 5 minutes; sprinkle with salt and pepper. Arrange frozen hashbrowns in a lightly greased 13"x9" baking pan; top with 2/3 of green onions and one cup cheese. Add sausage mixture; sprinkle with remaining cheese. Bake at 350 degrees until hashbrowns are tender, about 45 minutes. Garnish with remaining onions. Serves 6 to 8.

Enjoy a weekend retreat, at home
or away! Spend the day in your
jammies...savor a leisurely brunch,
work puzzles, re-read a favorite
book or browse holiday catalogs.
What could be cozier?

Autumn Apple-Walnut Pancake

Liz Plotnick-Snay
Gooseberry Patch

Oven-baked and filled with the best flavors of fall.

3 T. butter, divided
2 apples, cored, peeled and
    thinly sliced
1/3 c. brown sugar, packed
1/2 t. cinnamon
1/8 t. nutmeg
1/2 c. chopped walnuts, toasted

4 eggs, beaten
1 c. milk
1 c. all-purpose flour
1 t. baking powder
Garnish: powdered sugar,
    maple syrup

Melt 2 tablespoons butter over medium heat in a large oven-proof skillet. Add apples, sugar and spices; cook and stir until apples are soft and just golden, about 7 minutes. Add walnuts; cook and stir until apples are caramelized, 2 to 3 minutes. Add remaining butter; stir to melt. Remove from heat. In a large bowl, combine eggs, milk, flour and baking powder; whisk just until blended. Pour batter over apple mixture in skillet. Bake at 400 degrees for 15 to 20 minutes, until puffy and golden. Cut into wedges; sprinkle with sugar or drizzle with syrup, as desired. Serve immediately. Serves 4.

Top decorative urns
with plump pumpkins
for a quick & easy
doorstep welcome.
Orange pumpkins are
oh-so cheerful, or try
white Lumina
pumpkins for a ghostly
appearance.

Cranberry-Pumpkin Waffles

Kendall Hale
Lynn, MA

Oh my...these are so much tastier than ordinary waffles!

1/2 c. sweetened, dried
   cranberries
1 c. hot water
2 c. all-purpose flour
2 T. sugar
4 t. baking powder
1 t. salt

1 t. cinnamon
1 t. ground ginger
1-1/2 c. milk
1/4 c. butter
1/4 c. shortening
2 eggs
1 c. canned pumpkin

Combine berries and water in a small bowl. Let stand for 10 minutes; drain and set aside. Combine flour, sugar, baking powder, salt and spices in a large mixing bowl; stir with a fork until blended. Combine milk, butter and shortening in a small saucepan over low heat; cook until melted. Cool slightly. In a separate bowl, beat together eggs and pumpkin; stir in milk mixture. Add milk mixture to flour mixture; stir with a wooden spoon until well combined. Stir in berries. Ladle batter by 1/2 cupfuls onto a lightly greased preheated waffle iron; cook according to manufacturer's directions. Makes 4 servings.

Write it on your heart that every day is
the best day of the year.

-Ralph Waldo Emerson

Creamy Cinnamon Syrup

Sharon Demers
Dolores, CO

Scrumptious on fruit-filled pancakes or waffles.

1-1/2 c. sugar
1 c. milk

1 T. butter
1/2 t. cinnamon

Stir all ingredients together in a heavy saucepan. Cook over low heat until slightly thickened, about 12 to 15 minutes. Store in an airtight container; keep refrigerated for up to one week. Makes about 2 cups.

Maple-Pumpkin Butter

Wendy Lee Paffenroth
Pine Island, NY

A recipe handed down from Grandma...
delicious on toasted bagels and warm muffins.

3 c. canned pumpkin
1/2 c. brown sugar, packed
1/2 c. maple syrup
1/3 c. apple or pear juice

2 t. cinnamon
1/2 t. ground ginger
1/2 t. ground cloves

Combine all ingredients in a large saucepan over medium heat; bring to a simmer. Cook for 5 to 10 minutes, until well blended. Pour mixture into a 13"x9" baking pan sprayed with non-stick vegetable spray. Bake at 300 degrees for one hour and 15 minutes, stirring every 20 minutes, until thickened. Remove; cool slightly. Store in an airtight container; keep refrigerated for up to 4 weeks. Makes 4 to 5 cups.

Put away summer toss pillows for the season...set out warm & cozy cushions of flannel or fleece.

Creamed Eggs

*Laura Fuller
Fort Wayne, IN*

Spoon over buttered toast...real comfort food.

1/4 c. butter
1/4 c. all-purpose flour
2 c. milk

6 eggs, hard-boiled, peeled
   and diced
salt and pepper to taste

Melt butter in a large saucepan over medium heat; stir in flour.
Slowly add milk; continue stirring over medium heat. When desired
thickness is reached, fold in eggs and heat through. Add salt and
pepper to taste. Makes 3 servings.

Pink Hot Cocoa Mix

*Tammy Moody
Thomasville, GA*

This cocoa is my favorite...I like to keep it in a pretty jar.

25.6-oz. pkg. powdered milk
16-oz. pkg. strawberry
   drink mix

6-oz. jar powdered non-dairy
   creamer
1 c. sugar

Mix together all ingredients; store in an airtight container. To serve,
place one cup boiling water in a mug; add 3 to 4 heaping tablespoons
mix. Makes about 6 cups mix.

Use a linoleum craft knife to
carve swirling designs in pumpkins.
Since only the outer surface
is carved, there's no need to
hollow out the pumpkins...so easy!

Parmesan Breakfast Steaks

Susan Biffignani
Fenton, MO

Serve with scrambled eggs and hashbrowns for a hearty breakfast that will satisfy cool-weather appetites.

1 egg
1 c. Italian-seasoned dry
   bread crumbs
2 T. grated Parmesan cheese

salt and pepper to taste
1 lb. beef round tip steak,
   thinly sliced
1 to 2 T. oil

Whisk egg in a shallow dish; mix bread crumbs and cheese in another shallow dish. Dip steak into egg, then into crumb mixture to coat; set aside. In a skillet over medium-high heat, cook steak until tender and golden on both sides. Serves 4.

Recapture the childhood fun of choosing new school supplies
at the 5 & dime store! Pick up a fresh set of colored pencils
and a new sketch pad or blank book to take on nature hikes
or just jot down favorite thoughts and sayings.

Overnight Oatmeal

Tyson Ann Trecannelli
Fishing Creek, MD

Fill up the slow cooker before turning in for the night...
in the morning, you'll wake up to hearty, hot oatmeal.

2 c. milk
1 c. old-fashioned oats,
   uncooked
1 c. apple, cored, peeled
   and diced
1/2 c. raisins

1/2 c. chopped walnuts
1/4 c. brown sugar, packed
1 T. butter, melted
1/4 t. salt
1/2 t. cinnamon

Mix all ingredients in a slow cooker sprayed with non-stick vegetable spray. Cover and cook on low setting for 8 to 9 hours. Serves 4 to 6.

Milk & Honey Couscous

Melanie Lowe
Dover, DE

Look for this fast-cooking grain in the pasta aisle.

2 c. milk
2 T. honey
1 T. cinnamon
2 c. couscous, uncooked

1/3 c. dried apricots, chopped
1/3 c. raisins
1/2 c. slivered almonds

Combine milk, honey and cinnamon in a saucepan over medium heat. Bring to a boil; stir in couscous. Remove from heat; cover and let stand for 5 minutes. Stir in remaining ingredients. Serves 8.

Early risers will appreciate a crockery cooker of
Overnight Oatmeal! Set out brown sugar and a small
bottle of cream on ice so everyone can top their own.

Maple Cream Coffee Treat

Michelle Campen
Peoria, IL

Brown sugar, maple syrup, cream cheese...these are so good!

1 c. brown sugar, packed
3/4 c. chopped nuts
1/3 c. maple syrup
1/4 c. butter, melted
8-oz. pkg. cream cheese,
   softened

1/4 c. powdered sugar
2 T. butter
2 16.3-oz. tubes refrigerated
   big flaky biscuits

Mix together brown sugar, nuts, syrup and butter in an ungreased 13"x9" baking pan; set aside. Blend cream cheese, powdered sugar and butter in a small bowl; set aside. Separate biscuits and flatten each into a 4-inch circle. Spoon one tablespoon cream cheese mixture onto each biscuit; roll up and arrange in prepared pan, seam-side down, in 2 rows of 10. Bake at 350 degrees for 20 to 30 minutes. Cool for 3 minutes; turn out onto a serving plate. Makes 20 servings.

A striking fall bouquet is as close as your own backyard!
Look for late-blooming flowers, short branches of colorful leaves
and even interesting bare twigs to arrange in a tall vase.

Stuffed Banana French Toast

Jo Ann

Take just a little extra time for a breakfast that tells your family,
"You're special!"

4 thick slices country-style
   bread
1 banana, thinly sliced
4 eggs
1/3 c. milk

1 t. sugar
3/4 t. vanilla extract
1/8 t. nutmeg
1/8 t. salt

Cut a pocket in the side of each slice of bread without cutting all the way through. Stuff 6 banana slices into each pocket; set aside. Whisk together remaining ingredients in a shallow bowl. Soak bread slices in mixture, turning once. Heat a lightly greased skillet over medium-low heat. Cook bread until golden, about 2 minutes on each side. Transfer to an aluminum foil-lined 13"x9" baking pan that has been sprayed with non-stick vegetable spray; bake at 350 degrees for 8 minutes. Serve with warm Maple-Pecan Syrup. Serves 4.

Maple-Pecan Syrup:

1 c. maple syrup
1 T. butter
1 c. walnut halves

4-inch cinnamon stick
1 t. vanilla extract

Combine ingredients in a small saucepan over medium heat; simmer for 5 minutes. Discard cinnamon stick.

What a neighborly gesture...invite the family of your child's new school friend for a weekend brunch. Send them home with a basket filled with maps and coupons to local shops and attractions.

Overnight Pumpkin French Toast

Janice Miller
Huntington, IN

Brioche bread is my favorite for this recipe. You can bake this right away, but it's best if refrigerated overnight.

15-oz. can pumpkin
6 eggs, beaten
3 egg yolks, beaten
4 c. milk
1 c. whipping cream
1-1/2 c. sugar

1 t. vanilla extract
1 loaf bread, sliced 1-1/2 inches thick
Garnish: maple syrup, whipped cream, chopped nuts

Mix together all ingredients except bread and garnish. Arrange bread in a lightly greased 13"x9" baking pan; pour pumpkin mixture over top. Cover and refrigerate overnight. Bake at 425 degrees for about 30 minutes. Top with maple syrup, whipped cream and chopped nuts. Serves 6.

A fallen leaf is nothing more than
a summer's wave goodbye.

-Unknown

Cranberry-Cider Spiced Tea

Wendy Jacobs
Idaho Falls, ID

Share a cozy pot of this tea with your best girlfriends.

8 orange spice teabags
4 c. boiling water
2 c. unsweetened cranberry juice
2 c. apple cider
1/2 c. brown sugar, packed

4-inch cinnamon stick
4 whole cloves
1/2 t. ground ginger
Garnish: orange slices

In a large saucepan, place teabags in boiling water; steep for 3 to 5 minutes. Discard teabags; add cranberry juice, cider, brown sugar and spices. Heat almost to boiling, stir until sugar dissolves. Strain to remove whole spices. Pour into teacups; garnish with orange slices. Makes 8 servings.

Pick any late-blooming herbs in the garden and tuck the stems into a grapevine wreath. They'll dry naturally, keeping their sweet and spicy scents.

Swedish Coffee Cake

Peggy Marchese-Horne
Stoneham, MA

My Aunt Phyllis always used to make this on cool evenings. The scent of it baking takes me right back to when I was 9 years old, visiting her and Grandmother Sadie at their home on the lake.

1/2 c. brown sugar, packed	1 c. sour cream
1 t. cinnamon	2 c. all-purpose flour
1/2 c. chopped walnuts	1 t. baking powder
1/4 c. margarine	1 t. baking soda
1 c. sugar	1/2 t. salt
2 eggs, beaten	1 t. vanilla extract

Mix together brown sugar, cinnamon and nuts in a small bowl; set aside. In a large bowl, blend together margarine, sugar, eggs and sour cream; set aside. Combine remaining ingredients except vanilla in another bowl. Add flour mixture to margarine mixture; beat until smooth. Add vanilla; mix well. Pour half of batter into a greased tube pan; sprinkle with 3/4 cup brown sugar mixture. Add remaining batter; top with remaining brown sugar mixture. Bake at 350 degrees for 40 minutes. Let cool before turning out of pan. Serves 10.

Go out to greet the sunrise! Wrap warm breakfast breads
in a vintage tea towel before tucking into a basket...
add a thermos of hot coffee or tea.

Farmers' Scrambled Eggs

Dale Duncan
Waterloo, IA

Use fresh corn cut from the cob, if you have it...yum!

1 to 2 T. butter
2 c. frozen corn, thawed

9 eggs, beaten
salt and pepper to taste

Melt butter in a skillet over medium heat; add corn and cook until warmed through. Reduce heat to low. Pour eggs over corn; sprinkle with salt and pepper. Cook and stir until done. Serves 6.

Maple-Glazed Bacon

Lynda Robson
Boston, MA

Divine!

1/4 c. maple syrup
1 t. Dijon mustard

1 t. brown sugar, packed
1 lb. thick-sliced bacon

Combine syrup, mustard and brown sugar in a small bowl; set aside. In a skillet over medium-high heat, cook bacon in batches until browned but not crisp; drain well. Brush bacon with syrup mixture and turn over; cook over low heat for 2 minutes. Brush with remaining mixture; turn and cook an additional 2 minutes. Serves 6.

In late October or early November, plant flowering bulbs for springtime color...it's the ideal time! You'll find lots of daffodil and tulip bulbs in garden centers.

Honey Cream Spread

Jamie Barnes
Camden, NC

Pack in a small crock and tuck into a basket of muffins...deliver to someone special. What a lovely surprise!

3-oz. pkg. cream cheese,   1 T. honey
   softened   1 t. lemon juice

Combine all ingredients; mix well. Keep refrigerated. Makes 1/3 cup.

Creamy Apple Butter

Patti Rafferty
Levittown, PA

Serve with warm bread. Wonderful at breakfast...dinner too.

8-oz. pkg. cream cheese,   1 c. apple butter
   softened

Whip cream cheese and apple butter together until smooth. Keep refrigerated. Makes 2 cups.

Pack away summer linens with sachets so they'll be fragrant when unpacked in the spring. Place a spoonful of dried lavender on a pinked square of pretty fabric, gather into a bundle and tie with a satin bow. So sweet!

A weekend in the country...
gather family & special friends for a weekend treat!

A rustic cabin on the lake...go fishing, play board games and just get caught up with each other.

A small-town B&B...enjoy cozy quilts, well-loved antiques and the scent of fresh-baked muffins.

Grandma's house on the farm...she's always glad to see you and ready with a basket of your favorite cookies!

Can't get away for a whole weekend? How about...

The nearest park...pack a picnic, load the kids into the mini van and go on a fall leaf hike.

The homecoming game at your old high school...grab your best girlfriend and go, you know you've been meaning to!

Easy Cheesy Chili Dip

David Wink
Gooseberry Patch

A tailgating favorite!

1 c. onion, chopped	15-oz. can chili without beans
2 T. margarine	8-oz. pkg. shredded Cheddar
10-3/4 oz. can cream of	cheese
mushroom soup	tortilla chips

Sauté onion in margarine over medium heat until tender. Stir in remaining ingredients except chips; cook over low heat until bubbly and cheese is melted. Serve warm with tortilla chips. Serves 8.

Hot Mulled Cider

Glenna Tooman
Boise, ID

Headed for a hometown parade?
Tote along a thermos of this hot, spicy cider!

1 qt. water	12-oz. can frozen lemonade
4-inch cinnamon stick	concentrate
2 t. allspice	juice of 2 oranges
1/8 t. ground cloves	1/3 c. honey
1 gal. apple cider	1 teabag

Combine water and spices in a large saucepan. Bring to a boil; reduce heat and simmer gently for 30 minutes. Combine remaining ingredients in a large pitcher; mix well and add to saucepan. Simmer until hot; discard cinnamon stick and teabag. Makes 18 to 20 servings.

Gather wild hazelnuts, hickory nuts and walnuts in the fall...
fun for kids and a treat to eat!

Melani's Artichoke Dip

Melani Moore
Columbus, OH

This dip is so good, you'll want to eat it right from the oven...
but do let it cool just a bit first!

2 6-oz. cans marinated
   artichokes, drained and
   coarsely chopped
1/2 c. mayonnaise
1-1/2 c. shredded Parmesan
   cheese
1-1/2 c. shredded mozzarella
   cheese

8-oz. pkg. cream cheese,
   softened
1/2 onion, chopped
2 cloves garlic, pressed
salt and pepper to taste
Optional: 1-1/2 t. prepared
   horseradish
shredded wheat crackers

Combine all ingredients except crackers; spread in a lightly greased 13"x9" baking pan. Bake at 350 degrees for 45 minutes, or until bubbly and golden on top. Serve warm with crackers for dipping. Serves 8 to 12.

If you don't live in a small country town, adopt one.
Go for homecoming weekend at the high school and cheer
along with the local folks at the football game...what fun!

Corned Beef Pinwheels

Lori Collins
Garrettsville, OH

*These hearty treats were my husband's favorite when we were
first going together...they still are, 15 years later!*

1-1/2 oz. pkg. onion soup mix
2-1/3 c. water, divided
2 c. biscuit baking mix

3 T. butter, melted
15-oz. can corned beef hash
1/4 t. pepper

Combine soup mix and 2 cups water in an ungreased 9"x9" baking
pan; bake at 400 degrees until it boils. Set aside. Stir baking
mix, remaining water and butter together to form a soft dough;
knead 8 to 10 times on a floured surface. Roll out dough into a
12"x8" rectangle; spread hash over dough to within 1/2 inch of the
edges. Sprinkle with pepper and roll up jelly-roll style. Cut into 9 slices;
arrange slices cut-side down in pan over hot soup mixture. Bake for
an additional 30 minutes. Serves about 4 to 6.

Fall mums come in glorious shades of red, yellow
and orange...you can't have too many! Insert pots in
hollowed-out pumpkins to march up the porch steps.

Tangy Cranberry Meatballs

Luanne Cook
Dallas, TX

Guests will love these sweet-tart meatballs.

1-3/4 lbs. frozen meatballs
1.2-oz. pkg. brown gravy mix
3/4 c. whole-berry cranberry
   sauce
2 t. Dijon mustard

2 T. whipping cream
Optional: sweetened, dried
   cranberries, minced fresh
   parsley

Place frozen meatballs in a slow cooker; set aside. Make gravy according to package directions; stir in cranberry sauce, mustard and cream. Stir until well blended; pour over meatballs and stir to coat evenly. Cover and cook on low setting for 4 to 5 hours, or on high setting for 2 to 3 hours. To serve, use a slotted spoon to remove meatballs to a serving dish. Sprinkle with dried cranberries and minced parsley, if desired. Makes about 4 dozen meatballs.

Stir caramel topping into a mug of hot cider
for an instant warmer-upper.

Savory Cheddar Spread

Cheri Maxwell
Gulf Breeze, FL

Pack in a ceramic crock for a thoughtful hostess gift.

8-oz. pkg. cream cheese,
   softened
1 c. shredded sharp Cheddar
   cheese
1 T. Dijon mustard

3 T. bacon bits
3 T. green onion, sliced
   and divided
buttery round crackers

Combine cheeses in a medium bowl; blend well. Stir in mustard,
bacon bits and 2 tablespoons onion; transfer to a serving bowl.
Cover and refrigerate for several hours, until chilled. Let stand
at room temperature 30 minutes before serving. Sprinkle with
remaining onion; serve with crackers. Makes about 3 cups.

After a busy summer, it's great to get together with friends
in the fall. Keep it simple with a spread of hearty finger foods
and appetizers like Savory Cheddar Spread. Everyone will
enjoy sharing news and catching up with each other!

Gorgonzola & Walnut Spread

Pamela Stump
Chino Hills, CA

Whenever I take this spread to a get-together, everyone raves!
You can make it up to 3 days ahead of time.

4-oz. pkg. crumbled Gorgonzola
    cheese, divided
1/2 c. chopped walnuts,
    toasted and divided
8-oz. pkg. cream cheese,
    softened

3 T. half-and-half
1/4 t. pepper
pita chips, apple slices

Combine one tablespoon each of Gorgonzola cheese and walnuts for topping; set aside. Place remaining Gorgonzola cheese in food processor. Add cream cheese, half-and-half and pepper; process just until blended. Spoon into a shallow serving plate; stir in remaining walnuts. Sprinkle with reserved cheese mixture. Serve with pita chips or apple slices for dipping. Makes about 2-1/2 cups.

Spend the day at a barn auction. Take along a notepad & pencil, a sack lunch and most of all, your imagination! Look for cast-offs that can be put to new use...for example, a trunk can become an end table. You never know what you'll find.

Sugared Cranberry Trail Mix

Becky Richter
Yelm, WA

*Fill small bags with this sweet, crunchy mix
to take along on a leaf walk.*

1 c. whole almonds
2 c. mini pretzels
1 c. sweetened, dried cranberries
1 egg white

1/2 c. sugar
1/2 t. cinnamon
1/2 t. salt

Spread almonds evenly on an ungreased baking sheet. Bake at
350 degrees for 7 to 8 minutes, until nuts are slightly toasted. Cool
completely. Reduce oven to 225 degrees. In a large bowl, combine
almonds, pretzels and cranberries; set aside. In a small bowl, beat
egg white until foamy. Pour egg white over almond mixture and toss
until well coated. Combine sugar, cinnamon and salt in a small bowl;
sprinkle over top and toss until well coated. Spread evenly on a
greased baking sheet. Bake for one hour, stirring every 15 minutes.
Cool completely on baking sheet. Store in an airtight container.
Makes 5 cups.

Whip up cozy throws in bright red or russet plaid fleece...
simply snip fringe all around the edges. They're so easy, you
can make one for each member of the family in no time at all!

HOMETOWN
Homecoming

Scarecrow Snack Mix

Geneva Rogers
Gillette, WY

Toss in some pumpkin or sunflower seeds too.

1-1/2 c. pecan halves
1-1/2 c. golden raisins
1-1/2 c. chopped dried apples
1-1/2 c. chopped dried pears

1 c. sweetened, dried cranberries
1/2 c. sweetened, dried cherries
1 t. cinnamon

Mix pecans and fruits together; sprinkle with cinnamon and toss to coat. Spread on ungreased baking sheets. Bake at 200 degrees for 10 minutes. Cool; store in an airtight container. Makes 7-1/2 cups.

Hungry Bear Crunch

Abby Bills
Orleans, NE

This recipe is a quick & easy, delicious mix of flavors...it won a Nebraska State Fair purple ribbon for me!

1/3 c. cherry baking chips
1/3 c. sweetened flaked coconut
1/3 c. mini malted milk balls

1/3 c. sliced almonds
1/3 c. bear-shaped mini
    graham cookies

Toss together all ingredients in a large bowl; store in an airtight container. Makes 1-2/3 cups.

Autumn carries more gold in its pocket than all the other seasons.

-Jim Bishop

White Hot Chocolate

Susan Brzozowski
Ellicott City, MD

A smooth, chocolatey hot beverage...treat yourself!

4 1-oz. sqs. white melting
    chocolate, chopped
1-3/4 c. whole milk

1/2 c. whipping cream
1/2 t. vanilla extract
Garnish: marshmallows

Combine chocolate, milk and cream in a small saucepan. Cook over low heat until chocolate is completely melted, stirring frequently. Increase heat to medium. Whisk vigorously until mixture is smooth with small bubbles around edges; do not boil. Remove from heat; whisk in vanilla. Pour into mugs and top with marshmallows. Serves 2.

Take in a small-town parade for real hometown spirit.
Marching bands, horse-drawn wagons and antique cars...
what fun! Remember to take along a blanket to sit on, some
trail mix for munching and some mini flags for the kids to wave.

Malted Hot Cocoa

Samantha Sparks
Madison, WI

A hot, creamy beverage that's just a little different.

3 1-oz. sqs. bittersweet baking
   chocolate, chopped
1/4 c. boiling water
1/4 c. whipping cream
1/2 c. milk

1-1/2 T. malted milk powder
Garnish: whipped topping,
   crushed malted milk ball
   candies

Place chocolate in a small bowl; pour boiling water over chocolate. Let stand for 3 minutes. In a small saucepan, combine cream and milk over medium heat; bring to a simmer. Stir in malted milk powder; set aside. Whisk chocolate mixture until smooth; add to milk mixture and bring just to a boil. Serve immediately, topped with whipped topping and sprinkled with crushed candies. Serves 2.

Decorate a grapevine garland to wind around the front door.
Garland can be found at craft stores...use orange or yellow raffia
to tie on gourds, mini Indian corn and dried seed pods.
It'll look wonderful all autumn long.

Warm Blue Cheese & Bacon Dip

Jo Ann

Garnish with a sprinkle of extra chives and bacon crumbles.

7 slices bacon
2 cloves garlic, minced
8-oz. pkg. cream cheese,
  softened
1/4 c. half-and-half

4-oz. container crumbled
  blue cheese
2 T. fresh chives, chopped
baguette slices, celery sticks

Cook bacon until crisp in a skillet over medium heat. Drain bacon on paper towels; crumble and set aside. Add garlic to drippings in skillet; sauté until soft, about one minute. In a medium bowl, beat together cream cheese and half-and-half with an electric mixer on low speed. Stir in bacon, garlic, blue cheese and chives; spoon into an ungreased 8"x8" baking pan. Bake at 350 degrees for about 30 minutes, until lightly golden. Serve with baguette slices and celery sticks. Serves 6.

Watch for clever places to take snapshots out in the country. How about the whole family lined up in front of a cornfield or a big round hay bale? Later, photos can be turned into delightful holiday cards.

Mary's Hot Clam Dip

Mary Cooper
Spring Hill, FL

*So tasty! My children just love it and my husband
requests it every weekend.*

1/2 c. butter
1 onion, chopped
1/2 green pepper, chopped
1 t. garlic, minced
1 t. hot pepper sauce
1 t. dried oregano
1 t. dried parsley

2 6-1/2 oz. cans minced clams
1/4 t. lemon juice
1/2 c. bread crumbs
Garnish: grated Parmesan
   cheese
assorted crackers

Melt butter in a skillet over medium heat. Sauté onion, green pepper,
garlic and seasonings until tender; set aside. Combine clams and
clam liquid with lemon juice in a medium saucepan; bring to a boil.
Simmer over medium heat for 5 minutes; stir in bread crumbs. Add
clam mixture to butter mixture; stir well. Pour into a lightly greased
8"x8" baking pan. Bake at 350 degrees for 20 minutes. Sprinkle with
Parmesan; serve with crackers. Serves 6.

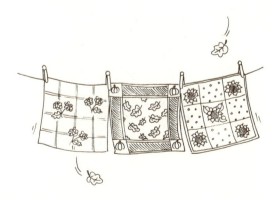

Vintage napkins can often be found at tag sales...use them
to wrap gifts from your kitchen or enjoy them on the dinner table!

Cranberry & Blue Cheese Ball

Kristie Rigo
Friedens, PA

This yummy, super-easy cheese ball is perfect for the holidays.

8-oz. pkg. cream cheese, softened
1 c. sharp white Cheddar cheese, shredded
4-oz. container crumbled blue cheese
6-oz. pkg. sweetened, dried cranberries
assorted crackers

Place all ingredients except crackers into a food processor; process until well combined. Shape cheese mixture into a ball on a length of plastic wrap; wrap well and refrigerate overnight. Let stand at room temperature for 30 minutes before serving. Serve with assorted crackers. Makes about 3 cups.

Savor a hometown church chicken barbecue, a school pancake breakfast or even an election day bean supper. There's always something tasty cooking in the country!

Smokey Salmon Log

Remona Putman
Rockwood, PA

Keep this scrumptious spread on hand in the fridge...
you'll be ready when surprise guests stop by!

2 c. canned salmon, drained and
    flaked
8-oz. pkg. cream cheese,
    softened
3 T. onion, chopped
1 T. lemon juice
1 t. prepared horseradish

1/4 t. salt
1/4 t. smoke-flavored
    cooking sauce
3 T. dried parsley
Optional: 1/2 c. chopped pecans
melba toast, assorted crackers

Combine first 7 ingredients; mix well. Shape into a log; wrap in plastic wrap and chill. At serving time, roll in parsley and pecans, if using. Serve with toast or crackers. Makes about 4 cups.

Carve an extra Jack-'O-Lantern or 2 and deliver to elderly neighbors so they can enjoy some Halloween fun...what a neighborly gesture!

Peanut Butter-Honey Popcorn

Travella Hershey
Temples, PA

Delicious...keeps for a long time too, if you can resist nibbling on it!

16 c. popped popcorn
1 c. sugar
1 c. honey

1 c. creamy peanut butter
1 c. salted peanuts

Place popped corn in a very large pan; set aside. Combine sugar and honey in a heavy saucepan over medium heat. Bring to a boil, stirring constantly; cook for 5 minutes. Remove from heat; stir in peanut butter and peanuts. Pour over popcorn; toss to coat. Pour onto wax paper and cool completely. Break apart and store in airtight containers. Makes about 20 cups.

Scenic vintage souvenir plates are fun to collect at flea markets.
Gather a variety from your home state or pick up plates from
coast-to-coast vacation spots. They're sure to spark
conversation at casual dinners with friends!

White Chocolate Crunch

Jody Stickle
Nashville, TN

*This can be frozen in plastic zipping bags...why not make a
batch now and save some for Christmas?*

3 pkgs. microwave popcorn,
   popped
16-oz. pkg. white melting
   chocolate

1/4 c. creamy peanut butter
2 c. salted peanuts
2 c. crispy rice cereal

Place popped corn in a very large bowl or roasting pan; set aside.
Melt chocolate; stir in peanut butter and melt again. Pour over
popcorn; add peanuts and cereal. Mix well to coat. Spoon onto wax
paper and let dry. Break apart and store in an airtight container.
Makes about 18 cups.

Cool-weather fun sparks appetites, so take along homemade
popcorn treats for everybody. Pick up some new paper paint pails
from the hardware store to decorate with paint or paper cut-outs.
Fill with popcorn and wrap up in clear cellophane...yum!

Spicy Sweet Potato Spread

Perry Mickley
Delaware, OH

Definitely not the same old spread...scrumptious!

1 lb. sweet potatoes
1 T. olive oil
1 T. tahini or creamy peanut
   butter
1 t. cumin seed, toasted and
   crushed
1 t. brown sugar, packed
1 t. salt

1/4 t. cayenne pepper
1/8 t. pepper
juice of one lemon
orange zest to taste
1 t. crumbled feta cheese
1 t. pistachios, toasted and
   chopped
pita wedges or bagel chips

Bake sweet potatoes at 350 degrees for 40 minutes, or until tender;
cool. Peel and coarsely chop sweet potatoes; combine with next
9 ingredients in a food processor. Blend until smooth and creamy.
Spoon into a serving bowl; sprinkle with cheese and pistachios.
Serve with pita wedges or bagel chips. Makes about 2 cups.

Set mini pumpkins on top of terra cotta flower pots...
line them up the front porch steps for a cheery welcome!

HOMETOWN
Homecoming

Brie with Hot Pecan-Caramel Sauce

Laurie Wilson
Fort Wayne, IN

An extra-special appetizer that's oh-so-easy to make.

5-inch wheel Brie cheese
1/4 c. brown sugar, packed
1/4 c. water
1/2 c. pecan halves
1/4 c. whipping cream
1 T. butter
baguette slices, multi-grain
    crackers

Remove and discard top rind of cheese; place on a large serving plate and set aside. Combine brown sugar and water in a saucepan over medium heat; bring to a boil. Reduce heat; simmer until mixture is dark brown and reduced by half. Remove from heat; add pecans and cream, stirring well. Return to a simmer; cook until slightly thickened, about 4 to 5 minutes. Remove from heat and stir in butter. Spoon caramel mixture over cheese; surround with baguette slices or crackers. Serves 4.

Everybody loves a tailgating party...and a small-town college rivalry can be just as much fun as a Big Ten game. Load up a pickup truck with tasty finger foods, sandwich fixin's and a big washtub full of bottled drinks on ice. It's all about food and fun!

Debi's Maple Hot Chocolate

Debi DeVore
Dover, OH

A little maple flavoring makes delicious cocoa even better!

1/4 c. sugar
1 T. baking cocoa
1/8 t. salt
1/4 c. hot water
1 T. butter

4 c. milk
1 t. maple flavoring
1 t. vanilla extract
12 marshmallows, divided

Combine sugar, cocoa and salt in a large saucepan. Stir in hot water and butter; bring to a boil over medium heat. Add milk, maple flavoring, vanilla and 8 marshmallows. Heat through, stirring occasionally, until marshmallows are melted. Ladle into mugs; top with remaining marshmallows. Makes 4 servings.

Save seeds from this year's garden to plant next spring...it's simple. Collect flowers and seed pods, then shake out the seeds onto paper towels. When they're dry, place seeds in small paper envelopes and seal in canning jars. Don't forget to label them!

Cool Cranberry Sparkler

Ellen Folkman
Crystal Beach, FL

Light and refreshing.

2 c. cranberry cocktail juice,
  chilled

2 c. sparkling water, chilled
1/4 c. red sanding sugar

Blend juice and sparkling water in a pitcher; set aside. Dampen 2 paper towels with cold water and place on a plate; spread sugar on another plate. Press the rims of 4 glasses onto paper towels to moisten, then onto sugar. Carefully fill glasses and serve immediately. Serves 4.

Cranberry-Orange Tea

Ann Fehr
Trappe, PA

A warm, cozy drink for a chilly autumn eve.

4 c. white cranberry cocktail
  juice

4 orange spice-flavored teabags

Heat cranberry juice in a microwave-safe bowl on high setting until hot, 3 to 4 minutes. Ladle into 4 mugs; place a teabag in each. Steep to desired strength; discard teabags and serve immediately. Serves 4.

Everyone must take time
to sit and watch
the leaves turn.

–Elizabeth Lawrence

Sweet Pumpkin Dip

Michelle Riley
Gering, NE

This is so yummy! It freezes well, so save any extra to enjoy later.

2 8-oz. pkgs. cream cheese,
    softened
4 c. powdered sugar
30-oz. can pumpkin pie
    filling mix

2 t. cinnamon
1 t. ground ginger
gingersnap cookies

Mix cream cheese and powdered sugar in a large bowl. Blend in pie
filling and spices; cover and chill. Serve with gingersnaps for dipping.
Makes about 9 cups.

Autumn weather can be so fickle, chilly one moment, then
balmy the next...so keep some apple cider on hand. Whether
it's served chilled or spiced and piping-hot, it's always refreshing.

Chocolate Chip Cookie Dough Dip

Judy Palkovic
Freedom, PA

Mmm...tastes just like real cookie dough!

8-oz. pkg. cream cheese,
   softened
1/2 c. butter
1 t. vanilla extract
3/4 c. powdered sugar

1 T. brown sugar, packed
1 c. semi-sweet chocolate chips
1 c. chopped walnuts
graham crackers

Beat together cream cheese, butter and vanilla with an electric mixer on low speed. Add sugars; beat until well mixed. Stir in chocolate chips and walnuts; serve with graham crackers. Makes about 4 cups.

Pumpkin Pie Cheesecake Spread

Julie Fella
Greece, NY

You'll probably want to double this scrumptious recipe!

8-oz. pkg. cream cheese,
   softened
2 T. brown sugar, packed

1/2 t. pumpkin pie spice
1/4 t. maple flavoring
vanilla wafers

Beat cream cheese until light and fluffy; set aside. Combine brown sugar and pumpkin pie spice; stir into cream cheese. Add flavoring; stir until well blended. Serve with vanilla wafers. Makes one cup.

Grab a girlfriend and head for a late-autumn farmers' market...
you'll find colorful fall produce, homemade apple butter
and maybe even fresh-baked cookies to share.

Rye Mini Party Pizzas

Lisa Payne
Saint Louis, MO

*A delicious make-ahead appetizer…bake as directed, then cool
and freeze. To serve, reheat at 300 degrees until heated through.*

1 lb. ground sausage
1 lb. ground beef
16-oz. pkg. pasteurized process
   cheese spread, cubed

1 T. catsup
1 t. Worcestershire sauce
1 to 2 loaves sliced party rye

Brown sausage and beef in a large skillet over medium-high heat;
drain. Add cheese and stir over low heat until melted. Add catsup
and Worcestershire sauce. Spoon meat mixture onto rye slices by
tablespoonfuls; arrange on a lightly greased baking sheet. Bake at
350 degrees for 10 to 12 minutes, or until cheese bubbles and bread
is crisp. Makes 12 to 15 servings.

Small-town harvest festivals are full of old-fashioned fun…where
else could you eat a pumpkin burger or cheer on an antique tractor
pull? Check with your state's tourism office for a list of seasonal
festivals and fairs in your area, then pick one and go!

Deli Reuben Spread

Ashlee Mitchell
Powder Springs, GA

Surround with sliced party rye or rye crackers for dipping.

8-oz. pkg. cream cheese,
   softened
1/4 c. cocktail sauce
1 c. shredded Swiss cheese

1/4 lb. deli corned beef, chopped
1/4 c. sauerkraut, drained
   and chopped

Blend cream cheese and sauce together until smooth. Add cheese, corned beef and sauerkraut; mix well and chill. Makes 2-1/2 cups.

Search yard sales for baskets in all shapes & sizes....
you can't have too many! Use them all around the
house to corral clutter like games, books and toys.

Buffalo Chicken Dip

Charlotte Smith
Huntingdon, PA

Yum! Tastes just like buffalo wings, but so much easier to fix.

3 cooked chicken breasts, diced
8-oz. pkg. cream cheese, softened
15-oz. jar blue cheese salad dressing
12-oz. bottle hot pepper sauce
12-oz. pkg. shredded Cheddar cheese
celery sticks, tortilla chips

Combine chicken, cream cheese, salad dressing and hot sauce; spread in a lightly greased 3-quart casserole dish. Sprinkle with Cheddar cheese. Bake at 350 degrees until bubbly and heated through, about 20 minutes. Serve with celery sticks and tortilla chips. Makes about 9 cups.

An oh-so-simple harvest decoration...roll out a wheelbarrow and heap it full of large, colorful squash and pumpkins.

HOMETOWN
Homecoming

Jen's Zesty Honey-Lime Wings

Jen Eveland-Kupp
Blandon, PA

Crisp party wings with a refreshing sweet-tart seasoning.

1/4 c. honey
juice and zest of one lime
1 clove garlic, minced
1/4 t. salt

1/4 t. pepper
1/2 c. all-purpose flour
3 lbs. chicken wings
oil for deep frying

Mix together honey, lime juice and zest, garlic, salt and pepper in a large bowl; set aside. Place flour in a large plastic zipping bag and add wings, shaking to coat. Heat one inch of oil in a large skillet over medium-high heat. Add wings in batches; cook until golden and juices run clear. Drain; place wings in honey mixture and toss to coat well. Serve hot. Makes about 3 dozen.

Plan a fall family outing to a farm. Many are open to the public for good old-fashioned fun like corn mazes, hayrides and pumpkin picking. You'll enjoy it as much as the kids!

3-in-1 Cheese Balls

Cheryl Nolan
Wanganui, New Zealand

*I always looked forward to my grandmother making
these cheese balls every holiday season.*

8-oz. pkg. cream cheese,
  softened
16-oz. pkg. shredded Cheddar
  cheese
2 T. milk
2 T. onion, finely chopped

2 T. Worcestershire sauce
1/4 c. coarsely ground pepper
1/2 c. crumbled blue cheese
1/4 c. fresh parsley, minced
1/4 t. garlic powder
1/4 c. pecans, finely chopped

Blend together first 5 ingredients in a mixing bowl until fluffy. Divide
into 3 portions, about one cup each. Shape first portion into a ball; roll
in pepper. Add blue cheese to second portion; mix well. Shape into a
ball; roll in parsley. Mix garlic powder into third portion; blend well.
Shape into a ball; roll in pecans. Cover cheese balls with plastic wrap;
refrigerate. Let stand at room temperature for 15 minutes before
serving. Makes 3 cheese balls.

Host a neighborhood spruce-up! Everyone can help
trim bushes and pull bloomed-out annuals...kids can
even rake leaves. End with a simple supper for all.

Jezebel Dip

Carol Hickman
Kingsport, TN

*This sweet and savory southern favorite is also tasty as
a dipping sauce for chicken or pork.*

8-oz. pkg. cream cheese
16-oz. jar pineapple preserves
16-oz. jar apple jelly
6-oz. jar prepared horseradish
4-oz. jar hot mustard
1/2 t. pepper
assorted crackers

Unwrap cream cheese; place on a serving plate and set aside. In a large mixing bowl, combine remaining ingredients except crackers; stir until just blended. Spoon over cream cheese. Serve with crackers. Makes about 3 cups.

Lisa's Prize Cheese Ball

Lisa Barber
Dallas, TX

I entered this easy recipe along with a very fancy, decorated carrot cake in a recipe contest at work. What a surprise...the cake came in second while the cheese ball won the grand prize!

8-oz. pkg. cream cheese,
  softened
2-1/4 oz. jar dried beef, chopped
1 bunch green onions, green
  part only, chopped
2-1/4 oz. can black olives,
  drained and chopped
Garnish: finely chopped pecans
  or fresh parsley
assorted crackers

In a medium bowl, blend cream cheese until smooth. Add beef, onions and olives; mix well. Shape into a ball and roll in nuts or parsley. Serve with crackers. Makes 2 cups.

Arrange blazing red autumn leaves on a clear glass plate,
then top with another glass plate to hold them in place...
so pretty for serving a cheese ball!

A bonfire cookout...
make the most of fine autumn weather with a
block party supper around your backyard fire pit!

Cozy mugs of mulled cider will warm both hands...
and tummies!

Serve sizzling sausages in toasted buns alongside
carry-ins of baked beans and hot potato salad...mmm!

Kids can roast hot dogs on long forks and toast
scrumptious fruit pies in pie irons. Afterwards...
s'mores, of course!

As the fire burns down, it's time to tell ghost stories
(or swap jokes and tall tales if little kids are present)
and admire the stars in the clear night sky.
Ahhh...autumn!

Indian Summer
PICNIC

Apple Valley Cider Stew

Fawn McKenzie
Wenatchee, WA

Hearty, savory stew...a real tummy-warmer!

1 T. all-purpose flour
1 t. allspice
1/2 t. pepper
1/4 t. garlic powder
1 lb. stew beef, cubed
3 T. oil
1 to 2 c. apple cider

2 T. catsup
3 potatoes, peeled and chopped
2 to 3 carrots, peeled and
    chopped
2 stalks celery, chopped
2 onions, chopped
Optional: 1/4 c. all-purpose flour

Place flour and seasonings in a large plastic zipping bag; shake to mix. Add beef to bag, a few pieces at a time; shake to coat. Heat oil in a large saucepan over medium heat and brown beef; drain. Stir in cider and catsup. Reduce heat to low; cover and simmer for one to 1-1/2 hours, or until meat is tender. Add vegetables; simmer an additional 30 minutes, until tender. If a thicker stew is desired, make a paste using 1/4 cup cooking liquid and 1/4 cup flour; stir until smooth. Slowly add to stew; cook until thickened. Serves 4.

The leaves fall, the wind blows, and the farm country slowly changes from the summer cottons into its winter wools.

-Henry Beston

Smokey Mountain Cabin Soup

Julie Kovach
Brunswick, OH

*I was given this recipe by a friend who has a cabin
in the mountains. It's become a family favorite.*

9-oz. pkg. au gratin potato mix
15-oz. can corn, drained
14-1/2 oz. can tomatoes with
  chiles

2-1/2 c. water
16-oz. pkg. pasteurized process
  cheese spread, cubed
2 c. milk

Combine potato mix with cheese sauce packet, corn, tomatoes and
water in a large saucepan; bring to a boil. Reduce heat; cover and
simmer for 20 to 25 minutes, stirring often. Add cheese and milk;
cook and stir until cheese is melted. Makes 4 servings.

Chilly-Day Beef Barley Soup

Shirley Condy
Plainview, NY

*The first cold day of fall, I put on a pot of this soup to simmer and
things seem much warmer! It's delicious served with crusty bread.*

1 lb. beef eye of round, diced
1 T. oil
1 c. celery, chopped
1 c. carrots, peeled and chopped

1 c. onion, chopped
28-oz. can stewed tomatoes
3/4 c. pearled barley, uncooked
9 c. water

In a large soup pot over medium heat, brown beef in oil; drain. Add
remaining ingredients; simmer over low heat for 1-1/2 to 2 hours.
Makes 6 servings.

Bandannas in autumn colors
of yellow and gold make perfect
oversized napkins for soup suppers.

Apple & Turkey Sandwiches

Katherine Murnane
Plattsburgh, NY

A nice quick supper dish...delightful for a ladies' luncheon too.

2 T. jellied cranberry sauce
2 T. mayonnaise
8 slices sourdough bread
1 lb. deli turkey, thinly sliced

1 Granny Smith apple, cored,
  peeled and thinly sliced
1 c. shredded Cheddar cheese

Mix together cranberry sauce and mayonnaise; spread evenly over bread slices. Arrange bread on an ungreased baking sheet. Divide turkey evenly among bread. Top turkey with apple slices; sprinkle with cheese. Broil until cheese is melted and golden. Serves 4.

If you like toasted pumpkin seeds, try toasting winter squash seeds too! Rinse seeds and pat dry, toss with olive oil to coat, spread on a baking sheet and sprinkle with salt. Bake at 350 degrees for 10 to 15 minutes, until crisp. Yummy!

Indian Summer
PICNIC

White Minestrone

Susanne Grace
Franklinville, NJ

*Garnish with a sprinkle of grated Parmesan cheese
and some chopped fresh basil.*

2 T. olive oil
1/2 c. onion, diced
1 clove garlic, halved
1 stalk celery, diced
46-oz. can chicken broth
1/2 lb. boneless, skinless
    chicken breast

1/4 c. canned diced tomatoes
1 c. frozen Italian mixed
    vegetables
1 c. frozen pea, carrot
    and corn blend
1 c. small pasta shells, uncooked

Heat oil in a large stockpot over medium heat. Add onion, garlic and celery; cook until tender. Add broth; bring to a boil. Add chicken and simmer until done, about 6 to 8 minutes. Remove chicken; cool and dice. Add vegetables to stockpot; cover and bring to a boil. Stir in pasta and bring to a boil; simmer until vegetables and pasta are tender, about 7 minutes. Just before serving, return chicken to stockpot. Serves 4 to 6.

Autumn is time for apple fun. Pick your own apples in an orchard, watch cider being pressed at a cider mill or go to a small-town apple butter stirring. Don't forget to taste!

Sandra's Creamy Butternut Soup

Autumn's most scrumptious flavors...in a bowl of soup!

2 onions, chopped
2 T. butter
1 T. olive oil
15-oz. can pumpkin
1-1/2 lbs. butternut squash,
    peeled and cubed

3 c. chicken broth
2 to 2-1/2 t. salt, divided
1/2 t. pepper
1 c. half-and-half
Optional: shredded Gruyère
    cheese, croutons

In a large saucepan over medium-low heat, sauté onions in butter and oil for 10 minutes. Add pumpkin, squash, broth, 2 teaspoons salt and pepper. Cover and simmer for 20 minutes until squash is very tender. Process mixture until smooth with a hand blender or in a food processor. Add half-and-half and reheat slowly over low heat; add remaining salt to taste. Top servings with Gruyère cheese and croutons, if desired. Makes 4 servings.

Top bowls of hot soup with popcorn instead
of croutons for a crunchy surprise.

Pumpkin Patch Stew

Tina Wright
Atlanta, GA

*A hollowed-out pumpkin would make a clever
soup tureen for this thick, meaty stew.*

1 onion, finely chopped
1 clove garlic, minced
1 T. dried basil
1 T. olive oil
2 lbs. pork tenderloin, cubed
28-oz. can diced tomatoes
15-oz. can pumpkin
14-1/2 oz. can chicken broth

1/2 c. white wine or
   chicken broth
1/2 t. salt
1/4 t. pepper
4 potatoes, peeled and cubed
1/2 lb. green beans, cut into
   1-inch pieces
4-inch cinnamon stick

In a stockpot over medium heat, sauté onion, garlic and basil in oil
until onion is tender, one to 2 minutes. Add pork; cook for 3 to
4 minutes, until lightly browned. Stir in tomatoes with juice, pumpkin,
broth, wine or broth, salt and pepper; bring to a boil. Reduce heat to
low; cook, stirring occasionally, for 10 minutes. Add remaining
ingredients. Cover; simmer for one hour, or until potatoes are tender.
Discard cinnamon stick. Makes 6 to 8 servings.

Small-town county fairs, food festivals, craft shows, swap meets...the
list goes on & on, so grab a friend and go for good old-fashioned fun!

Crockery French Dip

Jennifer Gubbins
Homewood, IL

With 3 boys, this oh-so-simple recipe is
a favorite in my busy household!

3-lb. beef rump roast
2 c. water
1/2 c. soy sauce
1 t. dried rosemary
1 t. dried thyme

1 t. garlic powder
3 to 4 whole peppercorns
1 bay leaf
6 to 8 hoagie rolls, split

Place roast in a slow cooker. Mix remaining ingredients except rolls; pour over roast. Cover and cook on high setting for 5 to 6 hours, or until beef is tender. Remove meat from broth; shred with a fork and keep warm. Strain broth and skim off fat; discard bay leaf. Spoon shredded meat onto rolls and serve with broth for dipping.
Serves 6 to 8.

Make a gourd garland to hang on the mantel. Choose brightly colored mini gourds with long necks. Tie them onto a length of jute, leaving a few inches of jute between gourds...simple!

Old-Fashioned Veggie Soup

Mary Ann Dell
Phoenixville, PA

*Pack a hot thermos of this comforting soup for
a pick-me-up on your next fall leaf hike.*

3 c. vegetable or chicken broth
1-1/2 t. tomato paste
1/4 c. onion, diced
1/4 c. carrot, peeled and diced
1/4 c. celery, sliced
1/4 c. potato, peeled and diced
1/4 c. green beans, sliced

1/4 c. corn
1/4 c. baby peas
1/4 c. baby lima beans
1/4 c. cabbage, chopped
1 clove garlic, minced
salt and pepper to taste
2 T. fresh parsley, chopped

Combine all ingredients except salt, pepper and parsley in a soup pot
over high heat. Bring to a boil; reduce heat to low and simmer for
15 to 20 minutes, until vegetables are tender. Add salt and pepper to
taste; stir in parsley. Makes 4 servings.

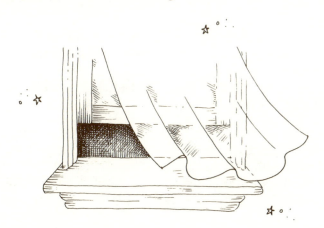

Leave the windows open on brisk nights in early autumn! The
cool breeze and night sounds of birds and crickets are delightful...
even in the city, it's easy to imagine you're out in the country.

Cheesy Wild Rice Soup

Tanya Graham
Lawrenceville, GA

Garnish with a little extra crispy bacon...yummy!

9 to 10 slices bacon, diced
1 onion, chopped
2 10-3/4 oz. cans cream of
   potato soup

1-1/2 c. cooked wild rice
2 pts. half-and-half
2 c. American cheese, shredded

In a skillet over medium heat, sauté bacon and onion together until bacon is crisp and onion is tender. Drain and set aside. Combine soup and rice in a medium saucepan; stir in bacon mixture, half-and-half and cheese. Cook over low heat until cheese melts, stirring occasionally. Serves 6 to 8.

Biscuit Bowls

Anna McMaster
Portland, OR

Homemade soup is even more special
when served in a fresh-baked biscuit bowl.

16.3-oz. tube refrigerated
   jumbo flaky biscuits

non-stick vegetable spray

Flatten each biscuit into a 5-inch round. Invert eight, 6-ounce custard cups, several inches apart, on a lightly greased baking sheet. Spray bottoms of cups with non-stick vegetable spray; form flattened biscuits around cups. Bake at 350 degrees for 14 minutes. Cool slightly and remove biscuit bowls from cups. Makes 8 bowls.

Start a delicious soup supper tradition on Halloween night.
Soup stays simmering hot while you hand out treats, and it isn't
too filling, so everyone has more room to nibble on goodies!

Baked Potato Soup

Linda Stone
Cookeville, TN

*We love this hearty soup with all the flavors of our
favorite baked potato toppings...scrumptious!*

3 lbs. redskin potatoes, cubed
1/4 c. margarine
1/4 c. all-purpose flour
2 qts. half-and-half
16-oz. pkg. pasteurized process
   cheese spread, melted

1 t. hot pepper sauce
white pepper and garlic powder
   to taste
Garnish: crumbled bacon,
   shredded Cheddar cheese,
   snipped fresh chives

Cover potatoes with water in a large saucepan; bring to a boil. Boil for
10 minutes, until almost cooked; drain and set aside. Melt margarine
in a large Dutch oven; add flour, mixing until smooth. Gradually add
half-and-half, stirring constantly over low heat. Continue to stir until
smooth and beginning to thicken. Add melted cheese; stir well. Add
potatoes, sauce and seasonings. Cover and simmer over low heat for
30 minutes. Sprinkle with garnishes as desired. Makes 8 servings.

Carve or drill a pattern of round holes in
hollowed-out pumpkins, then set tealights inside
for a flickering glow.

Baked Filled Sandwiches

Elaine Wilcox
Austin, MN

*This recipe was a customer favorite at the Gingerbread House,
the restaurant my sister and I owned together.*

1 loaf frozen bread dough,
   thawed
2 T. mayonnaise-type salad
   dressing
1/2 T. dried, minced onion
3/4 t. Italian seasoning

8 slices Swiss cheese
10 slices baked honey ham
10 slices roast turkey breast
1 egg, beaten
1 t. water
Garnish: sesame seed

Roll dough into a 14"x12" rectangle. Spread with salad dressing;
sprinkle with onion and seasoning. Make ten, 1-1/2 inch cuts on
each 14-inch side of the dough. Layer dough alternately with cheese,
ham and turkey, ending with turkey. Criss-cross the cut strips over
the top of the meat; place on an ungreased baking sheet and set aside.
Combine egg and water: brush over dough. Sprinkle with sesame seed;
let rise for 30 minutes. Bake at 350 degrees for 45 minutes to one
hour. Slice to serve. Serves 8.

Make leaf rubbings...it's fun and easy for the kids to make
wrapping paper and placemats! Arrange leaves face-down on
plain white paper and cover with another sheet of paper.
Remove wrappers from crayons and rub over the leaves...
their images will magically appear.

Hoagie Sandwich Bake

Penny McShane
Lombard, IL

So warm and cheesy...this is delicious! It makes a tasty appetizer too, if you cut it into smaller squares.

2 8-oz. tubes refrigerated
   crescent rolls, divided
1/3 lb. sliced salami
1/3 lb. sliced pepperoni
1/3 lb. sliced deli ham

1/3 lb. sliced Swiss cheese
1/3 lb. sliced provolone cheese
4 eggs, beaten and divided
grated Parmesan cheese to taste

Flatten one tube crescent rolls and press into a greased 13"x9" baking pan. Layer salami, pepperoni and ham over top of rolls. Top with Swiss and provolone cheeses. Brush half of beaten egg evenly over cheeses; cover with remaining rolls. Brush remaining egg over crescent rolls; sprinkle with Parmesan cheese. Bake, uncovered, at 350 degrees for 25 minutes. Cover with aluminum foil; bake for an additional 20 minutes. Slice into squares. Makes 4 servings.

Savor warm, sunny Indian summer days on the porch.
Spruce up your outdoor chairs or pull together mismatched
yard sale finds...it's easy! Spray paint them all the same
color or use a rainbow of colors just for fun.

Alabama Turkey Noodle Soup

Debbie Donaldson
Florala, AL

This is a wonderful use for leftover turkey. It makes a huge pot of soup and the leftovers freeze beautifully.

1 T. olive oil
1 yellow onion, chopped
1 bunch green onions, chopped
2 c. carrots, peeled and sliced
2 c. celery, sliced
2 cloves garlic, minced
10-3/4 oz. can French onion
   soup

6 c. chicken broth
1 t. poultry seasoning
1 t. dried rosemary
salt and pepper to taste
3 c. cooked turkey breast, diced
2 c. fine egg noodles, uncooked

Heat oil in a Dutch oven. Add onions, carrots, celery and garlic; cook until yellow onion is transparent. Stir in soup, broth and seasonings; bring to a boil. Reduce heat to medium; simmer until vegetables are almost tender. Add turkey and noodles; raise heat slightly and continue cooking until noodles are tender. Makes 8 to 10 servings.

An autumn soup supper is a wonderfully easy way to get together with friends & neighbors! Each family brings a pot of a favorite tummy-warming homemade soup...you supply go-withs like crackers, cider and a yummy dessert.

Hearty Sausage Soup

Wendy Dye
Monroe, NC

On cold nights, this soup is a family favorite!
Sometimes we'll vary it by using part Polish sausage
or hot sausage along with the Kielbasa.

1 T. olive oil
3 lbs. Kielbasa, cut into
    bite-size pieces
3 onions, diced
3 cloves garlic, minced
3 16-oz. cans kidney beans,
    drained and rinsed
3 14-1/2 oz. cans diced
    tomatoes, drained

14-1/2 oz. can beef broth
1/2 c. long-cooking rice,
    uncooked
.67-oz. pkg. fresh basil, chopped
1 t. Italian seasoning
1 t. dried oregano
1 t. dried parsley

Heat oil in a large stockpot over medium heat. Add Kielbasa, onions
and garlic and cook until golden; drain. Add remaining ingredients;
bring to a boil over medium-high heat. Reduce heat to low; simmer
for 1-1/2 hours, stirring occasionally. Makes 8 to 10 servings.

Balance a plump orange pumpkin on a cake stand
for a whimsical centerpiece.

Mini Turkey-Berry Bites

Jackie Smulski
Lyons, IL

Everybody will gobble these right up!

2 c. biscuit baking mix
1/2 c. sweetened, dried
    cranberries
1 c. milk
2 T. Dijon mustard

1 egg, beaten
6-oz. pkg. thinly sliced smoked
    turkey, chopped and divided
3/4 c. shredded Swiss cheese,
    divided

Stir together baking mix, cranberries, milk, mustard and egg until blended. Pour half the batter into a lightly greased 8"x8" baking pan. Arrange half the turkey over batter; sprinkle half the cheese nearly to edges of pan. Top with remaining turkey, followed by remaining batter. Bake, uncovered, at 350 degrees for 45 to 50 minutes, until golden and set. Sprinkle with remaining cheese; let stand 5 minutes. To serve, cut into 9 squares; slice each square diagonally. Makes 18 mini sandwiches.

Pack a lunch and go on a walk. Be sure to take along a
pocket-size nature guide, a magnifying glass and a tote bag to
bring back special finds...you'll have as much fun as the kids do!

Andrea's Picnic Pie

Andrea Gordon
Lewis Center, OH

Great for tailgating!

1 round loaf crusty bread
1/2 lb. sliced provolone cheese
14-oz. jar roasted red peppers, drained
14-oz. can artichokes, drained
16-oz. pkg. mixed salad greens, divided
1 c. chopped black olives
Italian salad dressing to taste
1/2 lb. sliced deli turkey breast
1/2 lb. sliced salami
1/2 lb. sliced deli honey ham
1/2 lb. sliced Swiss cheese
1 red onion, thinly sliced
2 tomatoes, sliced
6 to 8 slices bacon, crisply cooked
salt and pepper to taste

Cut off top of loaf and hollow out to form a bowl, leaving at least 1/2-inch thickness around sides and bottom. Set aside top. Pressing as you go, layer provolone cheese, peppers, artichokes, half the greens and olives in bottom of loaf. Drizzle with dressing. Press and layer turkey, salami, ham, Swiss cheese, remaining greens, onion, tomatoes and bacon. Drizzle with additional dressing; sprinkle with salt and pepper. Replace top of loaf and wrap tightly with plastic wrap; refrigerate until ready to serve. To serve, cut into wedges. Makes 8 servings.

On your next fall picnic, gather the prettiest autumn leaves...they'll look splendid arranged under the glass of a vintage serving tray.

Curried Harvest Bisque

Kathy Grashoff
Fort Wayne, IN

*Drizzle with a little extra half-and-half for an
elegant beginning to a holiday meal.*

1 lb. butternut squash, peeled
   and cut into 1-inch cubes
5 c. chicken broth
1/4 c. butter
1/4 c. all-purpose flour

1 t. curry powder
3/4 c. half-and-half
1 T. lime juice
1/2 t. salt
1/4 t. white pepper

Combine squash and broth in a heavy 4-quart stockpot. Cook over medium heat until tender, about 15 minutes. Using a slotted spoon, transfer squash to a blender; purée until smooth. Stir broth back into puréed squash; set aside. Melt butter in stockpot; stir in flour and curry powder. Cook and stir over medium heat until smooth. Add squash mixture; increase heat to medium-high and stir until soup thickens slightly. Reduce heat to low; add remaining ingredients and heat through without boiling. Serves 6.

Easiest-ever sandwiches for a get-together...a big platter of cold cuts, a basket of fresh breads and a choice of condiments so guests can make their own. Add cups of hot soup plus cookies for dessert...done!

Creamy Root Vegetable Soup

Dawn Klinter
Plymouth, WI

The roasted veggies are so delicious either hot or cold that you may want to cook extra to enjoy later.

2 T. butter, diced
3 to 4 Yukon Gold potatoes,
    peeled and cubed
3 to 4 carrots, peeled and sliced
2 turnips, peeled and cubed
2 parsnips, peeled and sliced
1 rutabaga, peeled and cubed

1 to 2 leeks, sliced
2 to 3 cloves garlic, minced
14-1/2 oz. can chicken broth
8-oz. container sour cream
salt and pepper to taste
Garnish: sour cream,
    chopped fresh chives

Spray a 13"x9" glass baking pan with non-stick vegetable spray. Scatter butter in pan; arrange vegetables over top and sprinkle with garlic. Bake at 400 degrees for one hour, turning once, until vegetables are tender. Set aside. In a large saucepan, bring broth to a boil over medium heat. Spoon in 3/4 of the vegetables and purée with a hand mixer. Add remaining vegetables; heat through. Stir in sour cream; add salt and pepper to taste. Garnish servings with a dollop of sour cream and a sprinkle of chives. Serves 4 to 6.

Get ready for spur-of-the-moment picnics on sunny autumn days... tuck a basket filled with picnic supplies into the car trunk along with a quilt to sit on. One stop at a farmers' market for food and you'll be dining amidst fall color!

Philly Blue Steak Sandwiches

Liz Vogelsong
Cecil, OH

My family just loves these open-faced hot sandwiches. You might want to double the blue cheese sauce, it's that good!

4 beef cube steaks
1/2 c. crumbled blue cheese
3-oz. pkg. cream cheese
1/3 c. mayonnaise-type salad
   dressing

1 t. Worcestershire sauce
4 slices Russian rye bread,
   toasted
8 tomato slices
8 onion slices

Broil or pan-fry steaks as desired; keep warm. Blend cheeses, dressing and Worcestershire sauce in a small bowl; set aside. Place toasted bread slices on a broiler pan; top each with a steak. Spread one tablespoon of cheese mixture over each steak; top with 2 slices of tomato and 2 slices of onion. Broil until bubbly. Makes 4 servings.

October's the month when the smallest breeze
Gives us a shower of autumn leaves.
Bonfires and pumpkins, leaves sailing down...
October is red and golden and brown.

-Unknown

Indian Summer
PICNIC

Chill-Chaser Pork Stew

Kathy McCann-Neff
Claxton, GA

Warms you right up after an afternoon of raking leaves.

2 to 2-1/2 lbs. pork steaks,
   cubed
2 T. olive oil
2 sweet onions, chopped
2 green peppers, chopped
2 cloves garlic, minced

salt and pepper to taste
6-oz. can tomato paste
28-oz. can diced tomatoes
2 8-oz. cans sliced mushrooms,
   drained

In a Dutch oven over medium heat, sauté pork in oil until browned. Add onions, peppers, garlic, salt and pepper. Cover and simmer over medium heat until pork is tender. Add tomato paste, tomatoes and mushrooms; bring to a boil. Reduce heat to low; simmer for one hour, stirring often. Serves 4 to 6.

Create a Halloween scarecrow! Make a simple T-shaped frame
of 2x4's and dress it with an old shirt and trousers. For the head,
stuff a brown grocery bag with newspapers and paint on
a face. Top off your new friend with a straw hat.

One-Pot Spicy Black Bean Chili

Lisanne Miller
Brandon, MS

Serve with crunchy tortilla chips or a pan of warm cornbread.

1 onion, chopped
2 t. garlic, minced
2 t. olive oil
3 16-oz. cans black beans,
   drained and rinsed
16-oz. pkg. frozen corn
14-1/2 oz. can tomatoes with
   chiles
1/2 c. water

1-1/2 t. taco seasoning mix
7-oz. can chipotle chiles in
   adobo sauce
1 T. rice vinegar
1/4 c. fresh cilantro, chopped
1/4 c. reduced-fat sour cream
Optional: salsa, fresh cilantro
   sprigs

In a medium saucepan, sauté onion and garlic in oil for 5 to
7 minutes, until onion softens and begins to brown. Add beans,
corn, tomatoes, water and taco seasoning. Bring to a boil; reduce
heat to low and simmer for about 15 minutes, stirring occasionally.
Combine chiles in sauce and vinegar in a blender; process until puréed.
Stir chile mixture and cilantro into chili, adding more taco seasoning
if a spicier chili is preferred; heat through. Divide into soup bowls;
top with dollops of sour cream. Garnish with salsa and a sprig of
cilantro, if desired. Makes 4 servings.

Nippy fall evenings are a fine time for a backyard cookout. Hang
lanterns on the fence and in the trees for twinkling light...magical!

Creamy White Chili

Janelle Dixon
Fernley, NV

This chili has such a fabulous flavor with its blend of green chiles, cumin, sour cream and chicken.

1 T. oil
1 lb. boneless, skinless chicken
   breast, cubed
1 onion, chopped
14-oz. can chicken broth
2 15-1/2 oz. cans Great Northern
   beans, drained and rinsed
2 4-oz. cans chopped green
   chiles
1-1/2 t. garlic powder

1 t. salt
1 t. ground cumin
1/2 t. dried oregano
8-oz. container sour cream
1/2 pt. whipping cream
10-oz. pkg. corn chips
8-oz. bag shredded Monterey
   Jack cheese

Heat oil in a large skillet over medium heat; add chicken and onion. Sauté until chicken is cooked through; set aside. Combine broth, beans, chiles and seasonings in a large soup pot over medium-high heat; bring to a boil. Add chicken mixture; reduce heat and simmer for 30 minutes. Add sour cream and whipping cream; mix well. Top with corn chips and cheese. Serves 8.

Kids will love grilled cheese sandwiches that have
been cut out with a pumpkin cookie cutter.

Judy's Pizza Rolls

Sara Moulder
LaGrange, OH

My sister gave me this recipe years ago. The baked rolls freeze very well...just move them into the fridge to thaw during the day, then pop them in a hot oven to reheat.

1 lb. ground beef
1 onion, chopped
1 clove garlic, minced
8-oz. can pizza sauce

dried oregano and basil to taste
2/3 c. mozzarella cheese, cubed
8 hot dog buns, split

Sauté ground beef, onion and garlic in a skillet over medium heat; drain. Add pizza sauce, oregano and basil; lower heat and simmer for 30 minutes. Let cool slightly; stir in cheese. Fill buns with meat mixture; wrap individually in aluminum foil. Place on a baking sheet and bake at 425 degrees for 20 minutes. Serves 8.

On Halloween, tuck tealights inside paper bag luminarias
and line them up along the walk...the flickering light
will lead little trick-or-treaters right to your door.

Indian Summer
PICNIC

Rustic Italian Baked Sandwich

Robin Hill
Rochester, NY

*Have a cozy picnic with friends in front of the fireplace
on a chilly autumn afternoon.*

1 loaf focaccia bread
1/4 c. Dijon mustard
1/4 c. mayonnaise
1/2 lb. thinly sliced salami
1/2 lb. thinly sliced deli ham
2 8-oz. pkgs. shredded
    mozzarella cheese

1/2 c. hot pepper slices
1/2 c. green olives with
    pimentos, sliced
1/2 c. black olives, sliced

With a serrated knife, slice bread in half lengthwise, then crosswise
to form 4 pieces. Spread mustard over cut side of bottom pieces; spread
mayonnaise over cut side of top pieces. Layer bottoms with salami
and ham; sprinkle thickly with cheese and top with peppers and
olives. Add tops to form sandwiches. Wrap in aluminum foil; place
on a 15"x10" jelly-roll pan. Bake at 350 degrees for 30 to 35 minutes,
or until heated through. Slice and serve hot. Makes 8 servings.

Gather pine cones to make winter treats for the birds...
a fun craft for kids! Tie a hanging string to the top of each
pine cone, then spread with peanut butter mixed with
cornmeal and roll in bird seed. The birds will love it.

Old-Fashioned Ham & Bean Soup

Mary Beaney
Bourbonnais, IL

Just like Grandma used to make...well worth starting a day ahead!

16-oz. pkg. dried navy beans
2 meaty ham hocks or
   1 meaty ham bone
1 c. cooked ham, chopped
1/2 to 3/4 c. onion, quartered
   and sliced
3 stalks celery, chopped

1/2 c. carrot, peeled and grated
2 bay leaves
1/2 t. garlic powder
1/2 t. seasoned salt
1/4 t. pepper
1/2 t. dried parsley
1/8 t. dried thyme

The night before, cover beans with water in a bowl and let stand overnight. Cover ham hocks or ham bone with water in a large stockpot. Simmer over medium heat until tender. Remove ham hocks or bone from stockpot, reserving broth; slice off meat. Refrigerate reserved broth and meat overnight. The next day, drain beans and set aside. Discard fat from top of reserved broth; add beans, meat, and remaining ingredients to broth. Bring to a boil. Reduce heat; simmer until beans are tender and soup is desired thickness, about one hour. Discard bay leaves. Serves 4 to 6.

Prewarmed soup bowls are a thoughtful touch. Set oven-safe crocks on a baking sheet and tuck into a warm oven for a few minutes. Ladle in hot, hearty soup...mmm, pass the cornbread!

Shrimp & Corn Chowder

Carla Phillips-Puckett
Bristol, VA

Serve piping hot...wonderful with buttery toasted Italian bread.

1/4 to 1/2 c. onion, chopped
1 clove garlic, minced
1 to 2 T. butter
2 10-3/4 oz. cans cream
   of potato soup
1-3/4 to 2 c. milk

1/2 c. cream cheese, softened
1-1/2 c. uncooked small shrimp,
   peeled
8-oz. can corn, drained
pepper to taste

In a large saucepan over medium heat, cook onion and garlic in butter just until tender. Slowly blend in soup, milk and cream cheese; add shrimp, corn and pepper. Bring to a boil; reduce heat, cover and simmer for about 15 minutes, or until shrimp are cooked and pink, stirring occasionally. Makes about 6 servings.

I would rather sit on a pumpkin and have it all to myself,
than be crowded on a velvet cushion.

-Henry David Thoreau

Pork & Green Chile Stew

Vickie

Add more chiles if you like it extra hot...
serve a basket of warm flour tortillas alongside.

3 lbs. boneless pork loin, cubed
3 T. oil
4 c. chicken broth, divided
14-1/2 oz. can diced tomatoes
11-oz. can corn, drained
10-oz. jar green chile salsa
4-oz. can chopped green chiles
3 stalks celery, chopped
4 cloves garlic, minced
salt to taste

In a stockpot, brown pork in oil over medium-high heat. Remove pork and set aside, reserving drippings in stockpot; increase heat to high. Add one cup broth to reserved drippings; cook and stir until boiling. Return pork to stockpot; stir in remaining ingredients and enough of remaining broth to barely cover. Reduce heat to low. Cover and simmer for 1-1/2 to 2 hours, until thickened and pork is very tender. Makes 8 servings.

On clear, crisp autumn days, freshen household quilts and blankets for winter...simply shake them out and spread over a porch rail or fence. Sunshine and fresh air will quickly chase away any mustiness that they've picked up in storage.

Molawa Family Meatloaf

Janice Molawa
Spring Grove, IL

Our favorite comfort food...pass the mashed potatoes!

4 lbs. ground beef
2 c. quick-cooking oats,
    uncooked
4 eggs, beaten
1 onion, chopped
1 c. sliced mushrooms
1/2 c. green pepper, chopped

1/2 c. celery, chopped
1 t. garlic powder
1 t. salt
1 t. pepper
2 c. shredded Cheddar cheese
3/4 c. catsup

Combine all ingredients except catsup in a large bowl. Mix well and form into 2 loaves. Place in two, 9"x5" loaf pans; spread catsup over top. Bake at 350 degrees for one hour and 15 minutes. Serves 8 to 10.

Grilled Meatloaf Sandwiches

Darrell Lawry
Kissimmee, FL

*A family favorite...sometimes I'll make a meatloaf
just so we can have these cheesy meatloaf sandwiches.*

4 thick slices baked meatloaf
3 T. oil, divided
8 slices sourdough bread,
    divided

4 t. coarse mustard
4 t. catsup
4 slices Monterey Jack cheese

In a skillet over medium heat, brown meatloaf slices on both sides in one tablespoon oil. Spread 4 slices bread with mustard; spread remaining bread with catsup. Arrange meatloaf on mustard-covered bread slices; top with cheese. Top with catsup-covered slices. Heat remaining oil in a skillet over medium heat. Cook sandwiches on both sides, until golden and cheese is melted. Serves 4.

Pumpkin patch fun...
kids will love picking their very own pumpkins!

Dress kids warmly in mittens and caps...with rubber boots in case of mud. Take along a little red wagon to carry home their pumpkin bounty.

Look for pumpkins in all sizes, shapes and colors... round orange Magic Lantern, green striped Cushaw, tiny white Baby Boo and mammoth Big Max.

Check out all the other fun at the pumpkin farm... petting sheep and goats, going through the corn maze, maybe even climbing into a tractor-pulled wagon for a hayride!

Back home...turn kids loose with washable acrylic paints and markers in lots of colors to decorate their pumpkins safely and easily.

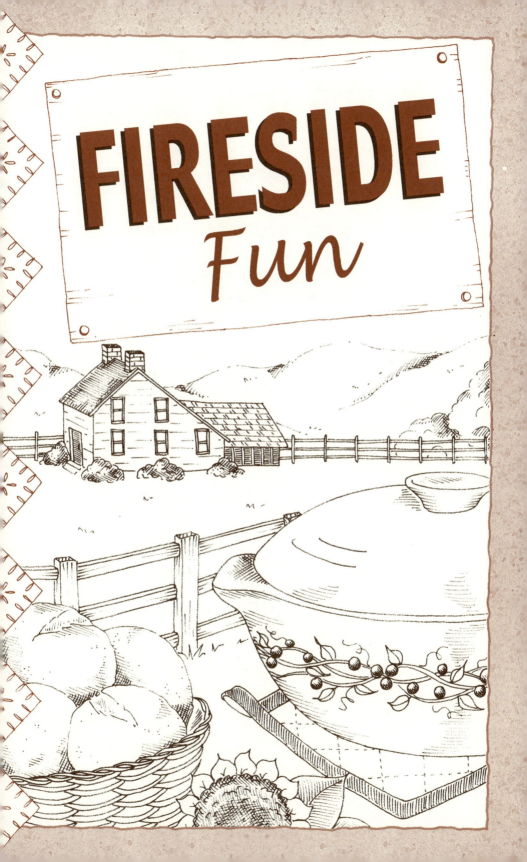

FIRESIDE
Fun

Apple & Sweet Potato Bake

Kathy Grashoff
Fort Wayne, IN

All the yummiest flavors of fall in one scrumptious dish.

4 c. apples, cored, peeled
   and sliced
4 c. sweet potatoes, peeled
   and sliced
2 t. onion, minced

3/4 c. apple juice
3/4 c. maple syrup
1/2 c. butter, melted
12 brown & serve pork
   breakfast sausages

Layer apples, sweet potatoes and onion in a greased 2-quart casserole dish; set aside. Combine juice, syrup and butter; pour over layered mixture. Cover and bake at 350 degrees for one hour. Arrange sausages on top; bake for an additional 15 to 20 minutes, or until sausages are browned. Serves 6.

Choose a crisp fall evening to gather friends around a crackling
campfire. Serve hot cocoa and cookies, tell ghost stories
and watch smoke spiraling up as the evening goes by...
could there be anything cozier?

FIRESIDE
Fun

Brown Sugar Acorn Squash

Carolyn Gonzales
Bountiful, UT

Try preparing sweet dumpling squash this way too.

2 acorn squash, halved and
   seeded
2 T. butter, sliced

2 T. brown sugar, packed
1 t. cinnamon
1/2 t. ground ginger

Arrange squash halves cut-side up in an ungreased 13"x9" baking pan. Place 1/2 tablespoon butter in each half; sprinkle with sugar and spices. Add about 1/2 inch of water to the pan. Bake at 350 degrees for one hour, or until squash is tender. Makes 4 servings.

Create a pumpkin man to greet visitors. Stack up 3 pumpkins snowman-style, removing stems and trimming bottoms as needed so they sit flat. Add twig arms and a whimsical face...fun!

Corn Muffin Sausage Stuffin'

Tonya Sheppard
Galveston, TX

Mom always baked up corn muffins to crumble for this dressing,
thus our pet name for it. Today I use cornbread stuffing mix
for a shortcut, and it's still tasty.

2 6-oz. pkgs. cornbread
   stuffing mix, prepared
1 lb. ground pork sausage,
   browned and drained
1 onion, chopped

4 stalks celery, chopped
2 T. butter, melted
1 t. poultry seasoning
14-1/2 oz. can chicken broth

Combine all ingredients in a large bowl. Toss lightly and spoon
into a lightly greased 13"x9" baking pan. Bake at 350 degrees for
30 minutes, until golden. Serves 10.

Bring out all your vintage bowls of wood, copper, yellowware and
rustic brown glazed ware. They go oh-so well with autumn colors
and look wonderful brimming with nuts, shiny fruit or spicy cookies.

FIRESIDE
Fun

Wild Rice Casserole

Vickie Rounds
Iroquois, SD

Feeds a crowd as a hearty side dish or even a one-dish dinner.

10-3/4 oz. can cream of
  mushroom soup
10-3/4 oz. can cream of
  chicken soup
1 c. chicken broth
2 6-oz. pkgs. long grain and
  wild rice, cooked
3-1/2 to 4 c. cooked chicken,
  diced

8-oz. can sliced mushrooms,
  drained
Optional: 8-oz. can sliced water
  chestnuts, drained
1-1/2 c. crushed potato chips
8-oz. pkg. shredded Cheddar
  cheese

Mix soups and broth together in a large bowl; add cooked rice and mix
well. Add chicken, mushrooms and water chestnuts, if using. Spread
mixture in a lightly greased 13"x9" baking pan. Top with potato chips
and cheese. Bake at 350 degrees for 45 to 60 minutes. Makes 12 to
14 servings.

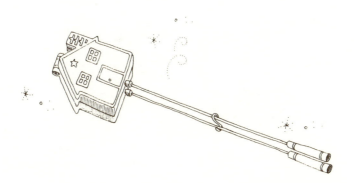

Stoke up a fire in the fireplace for a casual fireside supper. Toast
sandwiches in pie irons and make s'mores for dessert...so cozy!

Sweet Potato Fruit & Nut Loaf

Jo Ann Valentine
Oviedo, FL

The batter makes yummy tea muffins too.

1-1/2 c. all-purpose flour
1-1/4 c. sugar
1/4 t. salt
1 t. cinnamon
1 t. pumpkin pie spice
2 eggs, beaten
1 c. milk

1/2 c. oil
1-1/4 c. canned sweet potatoes,
    drained and mashed
1/2 c. maraschino cherries,
    drained and chopped
1/2 c. chopped pecans
1/4 c. golden raisins

Mix flour, sugar, salt and spices in a medium bowl; blend in eggs, milk and oil. Stir in remaining ingredients; pour into a greased and floured 9"x5" loaf pan. Bake at 350 degrees for 45 minutes. Makes one loaf.

Quick breads are tasty filled with fall's bounty of nuts and fruit.
For the tenderest muffins and loaves, don't overmix...just stir
the batter until moistened. A few lumps won't matter.

Apple Butter Loaf

Carol Hickman
Kingsport, TN

*Wrap a freshly baked loaf in a pretty
tea towel to welcome a new neighbor.*

2-1/2 c. all-purpose flour	3/4 c. apple butter
1 T. baking powder	1/4 c. oil
1/2 t. salt	2 c. milk
1/4 c. sugar	3/4 c. golden raisins
1 t. cinnamon	3/4 c. chopped walnuts

Combine flour, baking powder, salt, sugar and cinnamon in a mixing bowl, stirring to blend. Set aside. In a separate mixing bowl, stir together apple butter, oil and milk. Add apple butter mixture to flour mixture, stirring until well blended. Stir in raisins and walnuts. Pour batter into a greased and floured 9"x5" loaf pan. Bake at 350 degrees for 45 to 50 minutes, until bread tests done with a toothpick. Cool in pan for about 10 minutes before removing to cool completely on a wire rack. Makes one loaf.

All seasons are beautiful for the person
who carries happiness within.

-Horace Friess

Autumn Apple Salad

Laurie Wilson
Fort Wayne, IN

Crunchy and sweet...a delightful partner for any fall meal.

20-oz. can crushed pineapple
2/3 c. sugar
3-oz. pkg. lemon gelatin mix
8-oz. pkg. cream cheese,
    softened
1 c. apple, cored and diced

3/4 c. chopped nuts
1 c. celery, chopped
1 c. frozen whipped topping,
    thawed
Optional: lettuce leaves

Combine pineapple with juice and sugar in a saucepan over medium heat; bring to a boil. Cook for 3 minutes; stir in gelatin mix until dissolved. Add cream cheese, mixing thoroughly; cool. Fold in apple, nuts, celery and topping. Pour into an ungreased 9"x9" baking pan; chill until firm. Cut into squares; serve on lettuce leaves, if desired. Serves 6 to 8.

Pick up old clothing like hats, dresses and coats at yard sales
and flea markets. Heap them in a big basket or chest.
See just how creative friends & family can be, putting
together impromptu costumes at a Halloween party!

FIRESIDE
Fun

Festive Cranberry-Pear Salad

Jo Ann

*A tangy dressing is combined with pears and
walnuts for a refreshing tossed green salad.*

1/2 c. cider vinegar
1/4 c. cranberries
1/4 c. olive oil
2 t. sugar
1/8 t. salt
1/8 t. pepper
2 red pears, cored

2 heads romaine lettuce, torn
   into bite-size pieces
2 heads Belgian endive, chopped
1/2 c. plus 2 T. chopped walnuts,
   toasted and divided
1/2 c. crumbled Gorgonzola
   cheese

Combine vinegar and cranberries in a saucepan over medium heat;
cook until cranberries are tender. Remove from heat; add oil, sugar,
salt and pepper. Place in a blender and process until smooth; chill.
Thinly slice one pear; dice remaining pear. In a large bowl, toss
together greens, diced pear, 1/2 cup walnuts and cheese. Drizzle
with dressing and toss to coat. Divide among 8 salad plates; top
with sliced pear and remaining nuts. Makes 8 servings.

Pumpkin seeds are crunchy and tasty in cookies and breads...
sprinkled over salads too. Look for them year 'round in the
Mexican food section, where they're labeled as "pepitas."

Harvest Squash Bake

Jacqueline McKenzie
Carrollton, GA

A colorful and oh-so-easy dish to serve at Thanksgiving.

1/2 c. butter, melted
1 sleeve round buttery crackers,
   crushed
4 yellow squash, sliced
4 zucchini, sliced
1/2 onion, chopped

2 carrots, peeled and grated
8-oz. container sour cream
10-3/4 oz. can cream of
   mushroom soup
2-oz. jar pimentos, drained

Mix butter with cracker crumbs; spread half of mixture in a lightly greased 13"x9" baking pan. Set aside. Combine remaining ingredients; pour over cracker mixture. Bake at 350 degrees for one hour. Remove from oven; top with reserved cracker mixture. Bake for an additional 15 minutes, until golden on top. Serves 6 to 8.

Thread doughnut-shaped cereal on long pieces of string...
hang on tree branches for a bird feeder that's child's play!

FIRESIDE
Fun

Mary June's Eggplant Casserole
Mary June Germenis
Houma, LA

So good! Add a side of pasta tossed with
spaghetti sauce for a complete meal.

1 to 2 T. olive oil
1 eggplant, peeled and cubed
2 c. onion, chopped
6 cloves garlic, chopped
1-1/2 lbs. ground beef
2 8-oz. cans tomato sauce

1/2 c. grated Parmesan cheese
1 t. dried basil
1 T. Italian seasoning
Optional: additional grated
    Parmesan cheese

Heat oil in a large saucepan over medium heat. Add eggplant; sauté until tender. Add onion and garlic; sauté until tender and set aside. Brown ground beef in a skillet over medium heat; drain. Add eggplant mixture, tomato sauce, cheese and herbs to ground beef. Mix well and spread in a lightly greased 4-quart casserole dish. Bake at 325 degrees for 30 minutes. Remove from oven; top with additional cheese, if desired. Serves 8 to 10.

Bales of hay make comfy seating for a casual fall cookout.

Zesty Creamed Carrots

Debi DeVore
Dover, OH

A deliciously different way to serve carrots.

2 lbs. carrots, peeled and sliced
   1/2-inch thick
3/4 c. mayonnaise
1/3 c. half-and-half
1/4 c. prepared horseradish

2 T. onion, finely chopped
1 t. salt
pepper to taste
1/2 c. corn flake cereal, crushed
2 T. butter, melted

Fill a saucepan with one inch of water; add carrots. Bring to a boil over medium heat; reduce heat and simmer for 8 to 10 minutes, or until crisp-tender. Drain. In a large bowl, combine mayonnaise, half-and-half, horseradish, onion, salt and pepper. Stir in carrots; toss to coat. Transfer to a lightly greased 1-1/2 quart casserole dish; set aside. Combine cereal and butter; sprinkle over carrots. Bake, uncovered, at 350 degrees for 20 to 25 minutes, or until bubbly. Serves 6.

Bring out Mom's vintage Thanksgiving china early to get into the mood for fall. Use the bowls for soup suppers, the teacups for dessert get-togethers and even layer sandwich fixin's on the turkey platter!

FIRESIDE
Fun

Twice-Baked Potato Casserole

Teresa Stiegelmeyer
Indianapolis, IN

A much easier way to make twice-baked potatoes...
irresistible any time of the year.

6 potatoes, baked, cubed and
    divided
salt and pepper to taste
1 lb. bacon, crisply cooked,
    crumbled and divided
3 c. sour cream, divided

8-oz. pkg. shredded mozzarella
    cheese, divided
8-oz. pkg. shredded Cheddar
    cheese, divided
Garnish: 2 green onions,
    chopped

Place half of cubed potatoes in a greased 13"x9" baking pan; sprinkle with salt and pepper. Top with half each of bacon, sour cream and cheeses; repeat layers. Bake for 350 degrees for 20 minutes. Sprinkle with green onions before serving. Serves 8.

Take a short drive into the country and go stargazing on a frosty autumn night. Late October and mid-November are especially good times to see shooting stars, but any clear night will provide a world of wonder overhead.

Spicy Pear Bread

Amanda Homan
Gooseberry Patch

This fruit bread is really luscious! Spread with softened cream cheese for an extra special treat.

2 c. brown sugar, packed
1 c. oil
1/4 c. molasses
3 eggs, beaten
1 t. baking soda
1-1/4 t. salt
1-1/2 t. cinnamon

1-1/2 t. ground ginger
1/4 t. allspice
3/4 t. ground cloves
4 pears, cored, peeled and
    thinly sliced
3 c. all-purpose flour

Combine brown sugar, oil, molasses and eggs in a large bowl; mix well and set aside. Mix together baking soda, salt and spices; add to brown sugar mixture. Stir in pears, coating evenly; stir in flour. Pour batter into two, well-greased 9"x5" loaf pans. Bake at 350 degrees for 55 to 65 minutes. Cool for 10 minutes; turn out onto a wire rack and cool completely. Makes 2 loaves.

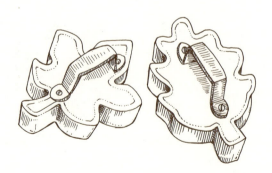

Make leaf-shaped butter pats...so pretty on the table at Thanksgiving. Simply slice chilled butter into pats and cut out with leaf-shaped mini cookie cutters.

FIRESIDE
Fun

Chocolate Chippy Pumpkin Bread

Linda Vogt
Las Vegas, NV

What could be tastier than pumpkin bread?
Pumpkin bread with chocolate chips, of course!

3 c. all-purpose flour
1 t. baking soda
1 t. salt
2 t. cinnamon
4 eggs

2 c. sugar
15-oz. can pumpkin
1-1/4 c. oil
1-1/2 c. semi-sweet
    chocolate chips

Combine flour, baking soda, salt and cinnamon in a large bowl; set aside. Beat together eggs, sugar, pumpkin and oil in a large bowl; stir into dry ingredients just until moistened. Fold in chocolate chips; pour into two, greased 8"x4" loaf pans. Bake at 350 degrees for 60 to 70 minutes, or until a toothpick tests clean. Cool for 10 minutes before removing to wire racks to finish cooling. Makes 2 loaves.

Cooked, mashed sweet potatoes, pumpkin and butternut squash
can be used interchangeably in quick breads, pies, soups and
other fall dishes. Feel free to substitute one for the other,
or give a new twist to a tried & true recipe.

Spiced Cranberry Sauce

Dianna Pindell
Powell, OH

Oh-so-easy to make! Serve it warm or cold...it's yummy either way.

1 c. water
1 c. brown sugar, packed
1/4 t. ground cloves
12-oz. pkg. cranberries

8-oz. can pineapple tidbits,
   drained
3/4 c. chopped pecans

Combine water, brown sugar, cloves and cranberries in a medium saucepan; bring to a boil over medium heat. Continue to boil until most cranberries pop, stirring often, about 7 to 10 minutes. Remove from heat; stir in pineapple and pecans. Makes about 3-1/2 cups.

Create a beautiful fall centerpiece in a snap! Hot glue brightly colored ears of mini Indian corn around a terra cotta pot and set a vase of orange or yellow mums in the center.

FIRESIDE
Fun

Slow-Cooker Warm Fruit Compote
Annette Ingram
Grand Rapids, MI

*Serve with a sliced baked ham for a sweet
and satisfying cool-weather buffet.*

21-oz. can cherry pie filling
20-oz. jar chunky applesauce
8-oz. can pineapple chunks
15-oz. can sliced peaches,
    drained

11-oz. can mandarin oranges,
    drained
1/2 c. brown sugar, packed
1 t. cinnamon

Combine all ingredients in a slow cooker; mix well. Cover and cook
on low setting for 1-1/2 hours. Serves 12.

Warm up for winter...start that knitting class you've been
meaning to take. Practice squares can easily be stitched
together into cozy scarves that will be much appreciated
by charitable groups.

Crispy Corn Fritters

Lara Shore
Independence, MO

Tender and golden, a real old-fashioned treat!

5 eggs
1/2 c. milk
2-1/2 c. all-purpose flour
1/4 c. baking powder
1/4 c. sugar
1/4 t. salt

1/4 c. butter, melted
1 c. creamed corn
oil for deep frying
Garnish: maple syrup
    or powdered sugar

Beat together eggs and milk; set aside. Combine flour, baking powder, sugar and salt. Add to egg mixture; mix well. Stir in butter; fold in creamed corn and set aside. In a deep saucepan, heat oil for deep frying to 375 degrees. Drop batter by tablespoonfuls a few at a time into hot oil; fry until golden, 3 to 4 minutes. Drain on paper towels. Serve warm with maple syrup or sprinkled with powdered sugar. Serves 10.

Make color-changing firestarters for the fireplace! Spoon 1/2 inch of powdered alum into mini paper cups and carefully fill with melted wax. Stir to mix and let set. Toss a cup or 2 into a fire and watch as green flames appear...kids love it!

FIRESIDE
Fun

Spicy Butternut Bake

Linda Roper
Pine Mountain, GA

Try using frozen butternut squash for this yummy casserole...much easier than cutting up a fresh butternut squash.

2 c. butternut squash, cooked
   and mashed
3 eggs, beaten
1 c. milk

1/4 c. butter, melted
3/4 c. sugar
1 t. ground ginger
1 t. cinnamon

Combine all ingredients in a large bowl; spread in a lightly greased 8"x8" baking pan. Bake at 350 degrees for 40 minutes; stir and return to oven. Bake for an additional 10 minutes. Serves 4.

Enjoy a movie night at home on a chilly autumn evening...
fun for the whole family! Let the kids each invite a special friend
and scatter plump cushions on the floor for extra seating.
Pass the popcorn, please!

Barchent Family Dressing

Debra Manley
Bowling Green, OH

*This recipe has been in my family for at least 100 years!
It's a "must" for us at Thanksgiving and Christmas.*

1 loaf white bread, torn
1/2 lb. ground beef, browned
   and drained
1/2 lb. ground pork, browned
   and drained
4 to 6 stalks celery, chopped

1 onion, chopped
1 c. chopped pecans or chestnuts
1/2 c. green olives with
   pimentos, chopped
salt and pepper to taste
16-oz. can chicken broth

Combine all ingredients except broth in a large bowl. Add broth and
mix just until moistened. Spread in a greased 2-quart casserole dish;
bake, covered, at 350 degrees for one hour. Serves 8.

How much dressing to fix when stuffing a turkey?
Here's a simple rule of thumb...for every pound of turkey,
figure on 1/2 cup of stuffing.

FIRESIDE
Fun

Old-Fashioned Sweet Potato Pudding

Laurie Walls
Spring Hill, TN

Stir in some pecans or golden raisins if you like.

3 c. sweet potatoes, peeled
    and grated
1 c. milk, warmed
1 c. sugar
1/2 c. butter

3 eggs, beaten
1 t. cinnamon
1 t. vanilla extract
1/8 t. salt

Stir together sweet potatoes and milk in a large bowl. Add remaining ingredients; mix well. Pour into a lightly greased 10" pie plate; bake at 350 degrees for one hour, until golden. Serves 6.

Light the front walk with canning-jar luminarias on Halloween!
Paint scary or funny faces on jars using black poster paint
and nestle tealights in several inches of sand.

Orange-Maple Glazed Yams

Roberta Miller
Washington, DC

Not your usual marshmallow-topped yams!

4-3/4 lbs. yams, peeled and
    cut into one-inch cubes
3/4 c. maple syrup

6 T. butter, melted
1-1/2 t. orange zest

Cook yams in boiling water for 3 minutes; drain. Place in a lightly greased 13"x9" baking pan; set aside. Blend syrup, butter and zest; pour over yams. Bake at 350 degrees for 30 minutes, stirring and basting occasionally with syrup mixture. Continue baking for about 15 minutes, until a glaze forms. Serves 8 to 10.

The goldenrod is yellow,
The corn is turning brown...
The trees in apple orchards
With fruit are bending down.

-Helen Hunt Jackson

FIRESIDE
Fun

Mack's Honey Apple Rings

Vickie Roddie
Evergreen, CO

A scrumptious garnish for pork chops or sausages.

1/2 c. honey
2 T. vinegar
1/4 t. salt

1/4 t. cinnamon
4 Golden Delicious apples, cored
and cut into 1/2-inch rings

Combine honey, vinegar, salt and cinnamon in a large skillet; bring
to a boil over medium heat. Add apple rings; reduce heat and simmer
8 to 10 minutes until tender, turning apples once. Serves 4.

Set a short pillar candle on a food can inside a clear glass punch
bowl, then fill the bowl with shiny apples...a lovely centerpiece
in a snap for an autumn dinner table.

Holiday Dinner Rolls

Athena Colegrove
Big Springs, TX

Serve warm with honey or homemade preserves...yum!

1 env. active dry yeast
1/2 c. warm water
1/3 c. plus 2 T. sugar, divided
1 t. baking powder
1 c. milk

1/3 c. margarine
1/8 t. salt
2 eggs, beaten
4-1/2 c. all-purpose flour

Dissolve yeast in warm water, between 110 and 115 degrees. Add one tablespoon sugar and baking powder; let stand for 20 minutes. Heat milk just to boiling; add margarine, remaining sugar and salt. Cool slightly; stir in eggs. Stir in flour; cover and refrigerate overnight. Two hours before serving, divide dough into thirds. Roll each third into 9-inch circles on a floured surface. Sprinkle dough with additional flour to prevent it from becoming too sticky. Cut each circle into 8 wedges. Form crescent rolls by starting at the wide end and rolling up. Place rolls on greased baking sheets. Bake at 425 degrees for 8 to 10 minutes. Makes 2 dozen.

Decorate paper placemats with leaf prints...so easy, kids can do it.
Brush leaves with a little poster paint and carefully lay in place.
Cover with a paper towel and roll lightly with a rolling pin.
Remove the towel, pull off the leaves...so pretty!

FIRESIDE
Fun

Mom's Sweet Potato Biscuits

Nancy Wise
Little Rock, AR

Seems like you can never have too many sweet potatoes!

2 c. self-rising flour
3 T. brown sugar, packed
1/4 t. cinnamon
1/8 t. allspice
3 T. shortening

1/4 c. plus 2 T. butter, divided
1 c. canned sweet potatoes,
    drained and mashed
6 T. milk

Combine flour, brown sugar and spices in a large bowl; cut in shortening and 1/4 cup butter with a fork until crumbly. Add sweet potatoes and milk, stirring just until moistened. Turn dough out onto a floured surface and knead several times. Roll out dough 1/2-inch thick on a floured surface; cut with a 2-inch round biscuit cutter. Place biscuits on an ungreased baking sheet. Melt remaining butter and brush over biscuits. Bake at 400 degrees for 10 to 12 minutes, until lightly golden. Makes about 1-1/2 dozen biscuits.

Dress up plain toss pillows for the sofa...
simply tack on cheerful fabric thrift-store
finds like old handkerchiefs, or calico cut-outs.

Apple Orchard Salad

Cyndy DeStefano
Mercer, PA

A family favorite…it's the only salad my children will eat!

1/2 c. oil
1/3 c. cider vinegar
1/2 c. sugar
2 cloves garlic, minced
2 Fuji apples, cored, peeled
   and sliced

1 bunch green leaf lettuce, torn
1 bunch red leaf lettuce, torn
1 red onion, sliced
1 lb. bacon, crisply cooked
   and crumbled

Combine oil, vinegar, sugar and garlic in a small jar with a lid. Shake well and pour over apples; let stand for 5 minutes. Toss together remaining ingredients in a large serving bowl; add apple mixture and toss to coat. Serves 6 to 8.

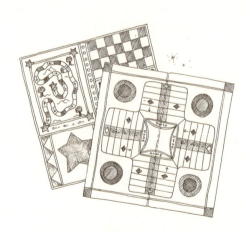

For fireside fun, pull out jigsaw puzzles, nostalgic
games like checkers, dominoes or card games
like Go Fish or Old Maid.

FIRESIDE
Fun

Crunchy Cranberry Salad

Debbie Donaldson
Florala, AL

Be sure to add the dressing right before serving...
you want the pecans and noodles to be crispy.

1 c. chopped pecans
3-oz. pkg. ramen noodles
1/2 c. red wine vinegar
1/2 c. oil

1/2 c. sugar
10-oz. pkg. romaine lettuce
1 c. sweetened, dried cranberries

Microwave pecans in a microwave-safe dish on high setting for 2 to 3 minutes, until toasted; cool. Break noodles into bite-size pieces; reserve seasoning packet for another recipe. Microwave noodles in a microwave-safe dish on high setting for 2 to 3 minutes, until toasted; cool. Combine vinegar, oil and sugar in a small bowl; mix well. At serving time, place lettuce in a large serving bowl. Add pecans and noodles; toss to mix. Drizzle with dressing; sprinkle with cranberries. Serves 8 to 10.

March pumpkins up a stepladder for a
quick & easy decoration on the front porch.

One Potato-2 Potato Mash

Jill Ball
Highland, UT

Two kinds of tasty potatoes are better than one!

2 c. potatoes, peeled and cubed
2 c. sweet potatoes, peeled and cubed

1/4 c. milk
1 T. butter, sliced

Combine potatoes in a large saucepan; cover with water. Boil over medium heat until tender; drain. Add milk and butter; beat until smooth and creamy. Serves 4.

Tuck some aluminum foil-wrapped apples or sweet potatoes into campfire coals for a treat. When they're tender, sprinkle with brown sugar or honey...eat right from the foil package.

FIRESIDE
Fun

Sauerkraut & Dumplings

Pamela Williams
Whitehall, PA

Delicious with roast pork.

16-oz. can sauerkraut
3 T. brown sugar, packed
2 c. water
salt and pepper to taste
1-1/2 c. all-purpose flour

2 t. baking powder
1/2 t. salt
3 T. shortening
3/4 c. milk

Mix sauerkraut, brown sugar and water together in a medium saucepan over low heat; simmer for one hour. Add salt and pepper to taste; set aside. Combine flour, baking powder and salt; cut in shortening and milk. Drop by teaspoonfuls into hot sauerkraut mixture; cover and simmer for 15 minutes, until dumplings are cooked through. Serves 4 to 6.

A quick fall craft for kids...hot glue large acorn caps
onto round magnets for whimsical fridge magnets.

Cranberry-Pecan Pumpkin Bread

Allison Paschal
Hot Springs, AR

My mother always baked this bread in large coffee cans,
now I use baby formula cans. I like to decorate the cans, put
the lids back into place and give them as gifts.

2 15-oz. cans pumpkin
2/3 c. milk
1 c. oil
4 eggs, beaten
3 c. sugar
3 c. all-purpose flour
1 T. baking soda

1/2 t. salt
1 t. cinnamon
1 t. nutmeg
1/4 t. cayenne pepper
1-1/2 c. chopped pecans
1-1/2 c. sweetened, dried
     cranberries

Mix together pumpkin, milk, oil, eggs and sugar in a large mixing
bowl; set aside. In a medium bowl, sift together flour, baking soda,
salt and spices; add to pumpkin mixture. Stir in nuts and cranberries.
Pour into three, greased 9"x5" loaf pans, filling 1/2 full. Bake at
350 degrees for one hour, or until done. Cool completely before
removing from pans. Makes 3 loaves.

Show off your pumpkin carving skills...set Jack-'O-Lanterns
on overturned large garden pots.

FIRESIDE
Fun

Sweet Cornbread

Crystal Myers
Hillsboro, OH

No bowl of chili or bean soup is complete without
a square of warm, buttery cornbread!

1 c. yellow cornmeal
2 c. all-purpose flour
1 T. baking powder
1/2 t. salt
1 c. sugar

4 eggs, separated
1 c. half-and-half
1 t. vanilla extract
3/4 c. butter, melted

Combine cornmeal, flour, baking powder, salt and sugar in a medium
bowl; set aside. Mix together egg yolks, half-and-half, vanilla and
melted butter in a separate bowl; add to dry ingredients and stir until
thoroughly moistened. Beat egg whites until stiff; gently fold into
batter. Pour into a greased 13"x9" baking pan; bake at 350 degrees for
30 minutes, or until toothpick tests clean. Serves 8 to 10.

Autumn hath all the summer's fruitful treasure.
-Thomas Nashe

Apple Cider Squash

Jill Ball
Highland, UT

Can't find banana squash at your grocer's? Try another
winter squash like butternut or Hubbard in this speedy recipe.

2 c. banana squash, peeled
   and cubed
1/2 c. apple cider
2 c. apple, cored, peeled and
   cubed

2 T. sugar
1/2 t. cinnamon
1/4 t. nutmeg

Combine squash and cider in a microwave-safe bowl; cover and cook
on high setting for 7 to 10 minutes, until tender. Add apple, sugar and
spices. Cook on high setting for an additional 3 to 5 minutes, or until
very tender. Serves 4.

Place feathered faux black crows in the windows, on lampshades
and all around the house for a spooky Halloween feel.

Nonny's Macaroni & Cheese

Rachael Gingras
Townsend, MA

My grandmother made this for years. It's not
traditional and that's what I love about it!

16-oz. pkg. ditalini pasta,
   cooked and divided
salt and pepper to taste
2 lbs. extra sharp Cheddar
   cheese, cubed and divided

2 16-oz. cans whole tomatoes,
   drained and divided

Layer half of pasta in a lightly greased 13"x9" baking pan; sprinkle
with salt and pepper. Add half of the cheese over top. Using your
hands, partially crush half the tomatoes and sprinkle them over
cheese. Repeat layers; cover with aluminum foil. Bake at 350 degrees
for about 45 minutes, stirring halfway through. Serves 6.

Early fall is the perfect time of year to spade up daylilies,
divide them and share extras with friends. They'll bloom
next year with renewed vigor.

Yummiest Taters

Peggy Market
Elida, OH

*These cheesy potatoes are quick to fix...and disappear
even quicker once they're served!*

7 potatoes, cubed
10 slices bacon, crisply cooked
   and crumbled
1 c. sour cream

2 8-oz. pkgs. finely shredded
   Cheddar cheese
1/2 t. salt
1/2 t. pepper

Place potatoes in a medium saucepan. Cover with water; bring to a
boil and simmer until tender, about 25 minutes. Drain potatoes and
return to saucepan. Add remaining ingredients; stir about 10 strokes,
until well mixed. Makes 6 to 8 servings.

Make spice-scented pine cones to heap in a bowl...
so sweet smelling. Simply dip pine cones in melted beeswax
(old candle ends will work just fine!) and while still warm,
roll them in cinnamon, cloves and nutmeg.

FIRESIDE
Fun

Smokey Spud Packets

Kay Marone
Des Moines, IA

Just right for a bonfire picnic on a clear autumn evening...roast some weenies on toasting forks and dinner is done!

1/3 c. olive oil, divided
2 lbs. new potatoes, thinly sliced
2 thin slices sweet onion,
   separated into rings

3/4 t. dried rosemary
1/2 t. salt
1/2 t. pepper

Brush half the oil on a 24-inch length of aluminum foil; top with potatoes and onions. Drizzle with remaining oil; sprinkle with seasonings. Fold over aluminum foil; seal edges firmly to form a packet. Place on a medium-hot grill or bake on a baking sheet at 375 degrees for 20 to 25 minutes, until potatoes are tender. Open packet carefully, allowing steam to escape. Serves 6 to 8.

Show kids how Grandma & Grandpa used to pop corn, in an old-fashioned hand-cranked popper on the stovetop. They'll love it!

Bring autumn's beauty indoors...
pick up materials for nature crafts on your next
leaf walk, maybe even in your own backyard!

Make bouquets of glorious red and gold leaves...before the first frost, cut small branches of colorful leaves. Tuck them into vases filled with water and 1/2 teaspoon glycerin from the drugstore. Refresh the water and glycerin once a week...leaves will retain their color for weeks.

Create an autumn wreath for the front door...collect all kinds of pine cones, seed pods and nuts and arrange them on a grapevine wreath. Hot glue in place and add a cornhusk bow...simple!

Make a harvest swag...wire together multicolored ears of Indian corn, tuck in wheat stems and tie on a homespun bow in seasonal colors. Hang small Indian corn swags on chair backs...charming!

Bountiful
HARVEST

Homemade Apple Pie Filling

Justine Reid
Hulett, WY

Savor the fun of a day at an apple orchard over and over...first when you pick the apples and again when you enjoy the delicious pies!

10 c. water
4-1/2 c. sugar
1 c. cornstarch
3 T. lemon juice
2 t. cinnamon
1/4 t. nutmeg

1 t. salt
2 to 3 drops yellow food coloring
5-1/2 lbs. apples, cored,
    peeled and sliced
6 1-quart canning jars
    and lids, sterilized

Combine all ingredients except apples in a large saucepan. Cook over low heat until thickened, stirring occasionally; set aside. Divide apple slices equally among hot sterilized jars; ladle thickened sauce over top, leaving 1/2-inch headspace. Wipe rims; secure with lids and rings. Process in a boiling water bath for 20 minutes; set jars on a towel to cool. Check for seals; attach instructions. Makes 6 jars.

Instructions:
Pour one jar filling into an unbaked 9-inch pie crust. Arrange a second unbaked pie crust over top; crimp crust and cut several vents. Bake at 350 degrees for 30 to 40 minutes. Serves 8.

Enjoy autumn's harvest! Late-season farmers' markets are overflowing with squash and root vegetables that are tasty in stews and casseroles... apples, pears and blackberries are delicious in pies and preserves.

Spicy Raisin-Pear Mincemeat

Doris Stegner
Gooseberry Patch

A family tradition at Thanksgiving and Christmas.

7 lbs. pears, cored, peeled
   and cubed
1 lemon, quartered
2 16-oz. pkgs. raisins
6-3/4 c. sugar
1 c. vinegar
1 T. ground cloves

1 T. cinnamon
1 T. allspice
1 T. nutmeg
1 t. ground ginger
9 1-pint canning jars
   and lids, sterilized

Coarsely chop pears, lemon and raisins in a food processor. Combine with remaining ingredients in a large kettle over medium heat; simmer until thickened, about 40 minutes. Spoon into hot sterilized jars, leaving 1/4-inch headspace. Wipe rims; secure with lids and rings. Process in a boiling water bath for 10 minutes; set jars on a towel to cool. Check for seals. Makes about 9 jars.

To process jars of preserves in a boiling water bath, set sealed jars in a large stockpot and add enough water to cover them by one to 2 inches. Bring to a boil for the amount of time specified, adding water as necessary to keep jars covered.

Tanya's Zucchini Jam

Tanya Payzant
Nova Scotia, Canada

A tasty solution for too-many-zucchini from the garden!
Tuck a jar into a basket along with some freshly baked
muffins for a welcome gift.

6 c. zucchini, peeled and grated
5 c. sugar
6-oz. pkg. peach gelatin mix

8 1/2-pint canning jars
and lids, sterilized

Put zucchini through a food grinder; pour into a large stockpot. Add sugar; stir well. Bring to a boil over medium heat. Reduce heat and simmer for 6 minutes, stirring constantly. Remove from heat; add gelatin and stir well. Spoon into hot sterilized jars, leaving 1/4-inch headspace. Wipe rims; secure with lids and rings. Process in a boiling water bath for 5 minutes; set jars on a towel to cool. Check for seals. Makes 8 jars.

Make jams & jellies for Christmas gift-giving during the fall,
when fruits are ripe and luscious and you have a little more
leisure time. You'll be glad you did!

Bountiful
HARVEST

Colorful Pepper Jelly

Judy Awe
Lincoln, IL

For a delicious cracker spread, stir 2 to 3 tablespoons of this spicy jelly into 8 ounces of softened cream cheese.

1 c. orange, yellow or red
    pepper, minced
1/2 c. jalapeño pepper, chopped
5 c. sugar
1-1/2 c. cider vinegar

6-oz. pkg. liquid pectin
5 to 6 1/2-pint canning jars
    and lids, sterilized

Combine peppers, sugar and vinegar in a large stockpot over medium-high heat; bring to a rolling boil. Boil for 3 to 4 minutes. Remove from heat; cool for 5 minutes. Add pectin, stirring constantly; let mixture stand for 2 minutes. Pour into hot sterilized jars, leaving 1/4-inch headspace. Wipe rims; secure lids and rings. Process in a boiling water bath for 15 minutes; set jars on towel to cool. Check for seals. Makes 5 to 6 jars.

When a recipe for jam or jelly calls for pint-size jars,
it's fine to use twice as many 1/2-pint jars instead.
However, when 1/2-pint jars are specified, don't use larger
jars, as the jam may not process thoroughly.

Horseradish Dill Pickles

*Amy Wrightsel
Louisville, KY*

The best pickles I've ever eaten! Not too hot, just enough to make them perfect with a grilled sandwich and a bowl of soup.

32-oz. jar kosher dill pickle
  spears
1/2 c. prepared horseradish

2/3 c. white vinegar
1/3 c. water
1-1/2 c. sugar

Remove pickle spears from jar and set aside in a bowl; drain pickle juice and reserve. Wash pickle jar thoroughly with hot water. Spoon horseradish into empty jar; return pickles to jar and set aside. Combine vinegar, water and sugar in a saucepan over medium-high heat; bring to a boil. Remove from heat; pour over pickles in jar. Add enough of reserved pickle juice to fill the jar. Shake jar vigorously to mix well. Refrigerate; shake jar every day for one week before serving. Makes one jar.

Look for pansies at the garden store to plant for an early touch of color in spring. Plant them in early November and blanket with an inch or 2 of mulch to protect from winter cold...in the spring, they'll pop right up!

Rosie Red Beet Pickles

Teresa Stiegelmeyer
Indianapolis, IN

We love to eat these pickles with salmon patties and cornbread.
Try them sliced on top of a tossed salad too.

2 c. sugar
3-1/2 c. white vinegar
1-1/2 c. water
1 t. salt
1 T. cinnamon

1 T. allspice
4 16-oz. cans small whole
    beets, drained
4 1-pint canning jars
    and lids, sterilized

Combine sugar, vinegar, water, salt and spices in a large kettle; bring to a boil over medium heat. Add beets. Reduce heat and simmer for 15 minutes; cool. Pack beets into hot jars; cover with liquid. Store in refrigerator up to 3 weeks. Makes 2 jars.

Oops, you got carried away and brought home too many fresh
veggies from the farmers' market! Save them by cooking up a big
pot of soup or stew and freezing it in meal-size portions.

Grandma Oakley's Corn Relish

Mary Oakley
Nashville, TN

*An old-fashioned hand-cranked meat grinder makes
short work of chopping the onions and peppers.*

12 ears corn, husked
4 c. sugar
4 c. vinegar
1 T. salt
12 onions, sliced
6 green peppers, sliced

6 red peppers, sliced
1 hot pepper, sliced
6-oz. jar mustard
9 1-pint canning jars and lids,
   sterilized

Slice corn kernels from cobs. Combine corn, sugar, vinegar and salt in
a large saucepan over medium heat; cook for 20 minutes. Grind or
finely chop onions and peppers; add to corn mixture. Stir in mustard.
Cook for an additional 20 minutes. Spoon into hot sterilized jars,
leaving 1/4-inch headspace. Wipe rims; secure with lids and rings.
Process in a boiling water bath for 10 minutes; set jars on towel to
cool. Makes about 9 jars.

Tag sales and flea markets are great places to find canning jars.
Check for cracks, buy new lids and save old-fashioned ones with
one-piece zinc lids for use as vases, tumblers or kitchen storage.

Bountiful
HARVEST

Garden-Fresh Mexican Salsa

Mary Murray
Gooseberry Patch

*There's nothing more scrumptious with your favorite Tex-Mex dish,
or served with crunchy tortilla chips for dipping.*

5 lbs. tomatoes, cored, peeled
  and diced
6 green onions, sliced
2 jalapeño peppers, diced
4 cloves garlic, minced
2 T. fresh cilantro, minced

1/2 c. vinegar
2 T. lime juice
4 drops hot pepper sauce
2 t. salt
4 1-pint canning jars
  and lids, sterilized

Combine all ingredients in a large saucepot. Bring to a boil over medium heat; reduce heat and simmer for 15 minutes. Spoon salsa into hot sterilized jars, leaving 1/4-inch headspace. Wipe rims; secure with lids and rings. Process in a boiling water bath for 15 minutes; set on a towel to cool. Check for seals. Makes about 4 jars.

Make freezer preserves...it's easy! Combine one pound ripe berries, 1-1/2 cups sugar and 2 tablespoons lemon juice. Bring to a boil, lower heat and simmer, uncovered, for 30 minutes. Spoon into sterilized freezer containers and freeze for up to 6 months.

Green Tomato-Pineapple Jam

Carole Anne Barbaro
Clayton, NJ

Everyone loves this different-tasting jam!
It's especially good with cold meatloaf.

4 lbs. green tomatoes, cored,
    peeled and thinly sliced
5 c. sugar
8-oz. can crushed pineapple
juice of 1 lemon

7 whole cloves
1 4-inch cinnamon stick
zest of 1 orange
6 1/2-pint canning jars
    and lids, sterilized

Combine tomatoes and sugar in a heavy kettle over medium heat;
bring to a boil. Boil until tomatoes are soft, about 20 minutes, stirring
often. Stir in pineapple; boil for 15 minutes. Add lemon juice and boil
until jam coats the back of a spoon, about 20 to 30 minutes. Spoon
into hot sterilized jars, leaving 1/4-inch headspace. Wipe rims; secure
with lids and rings. Process in a boiling water bath for 15 minutes; set
jars on a towel to cool. Check for seals. Makes about 6 jars.

Grandma knew this...before the first frost, pick any
green tomatoes that are still in the garden. Wrap each in
newspaper and store in a box at room temperature. They'll
ripen over the next few weeks, for one last taste of summer.

Orange-Cranberry Marmalade

Rosee Boehme
Boise, ID

During the Depression, my grandmother provided a home for older people in her sprawling 3-story Victorian house. She was very busy, yet always managed to find an hour just for me on early Sunday mornings. We would spend our time talking and Grandmother would make me hot cocoa and toast with orange marmalade. Now I'm in my 70's, and to this day, I still love orange marmalade.

6 c. oranges, thinly sliced
1 c. cranberries
1/2 c. lemon juice
6 c. water
1-3/4 oz. pkg. powdered pectin

9-1/2 c. sugar
1 t. butter
8 1-pint canning jars
     and lids, sterilized

Combine oranges, cranberries, lemon juice and water in a large saucepan over medium heat. Bring to a boil; reduce heat and simmer until tender, 45 to 60 minutes. Measure out 7 cups, adding water if needed. Stir in pectin and sugar; bring to a rolling boil. Boil for 4 minutes, stirring constantly. Add butter; stir until melted. Skim any remaining foam from surface. Cook for 5 minutes, stirring once each minute. Pour into hot sterilized jars, leaving 1/4-inch headspace. Wipe rims; secure with lids and rings. Process in a boiling water bath for 15 minutes; set jars on towel to cool. Check for seals. Makes 8 jars.

Give me juicy autumnal fruit, ripe
and red from the orchard.

-Walt Whitman

Apple Cider Chutney

Jennifer Eveland-Kupp
Temple, PA

Especially delicious with baked ham.

6 c. apple cider
1/2 c. cider vinegar
2 10-oz. pkgs. frozen
   pearl onions
1 c. apples, cored, peeled
   and chopped

1 c. raisins
1/2 c. brown sugar, packed
2 t. ground cloves
2 t. cinnamon
2 1/2-pint freezer-safe plastic
   containers and lids, sterilized

Mix together all ingredients in a large saucepan over medium
heat. Simmer, stirring occasionally, until mixture is the consistency of
syrup, about 30 to 35 minutes. Spoon into sterilized containers,
leaving 1/2-inch headspace; secure lids and freeze. Thaw in refrigerator before serving; keep refrigerated up to 4 weeks after opening.
Makes 2 containers.

Is your kitchen too warm in summer for making jams & jellies?
Stock up on ripe berries and freeze them to preserve in
cooler months. Freeze whole berries in a single layer on a
baking sheet, then transfer to plastic freezer bags.
They'll stay fresh and yummy for months.

Cowboy "Candy"

Deatra Flanagan
Terryville, CT

You'll love this sweet-hot sauce on just about anything!
Be sure to wear rubber gloves when slicing the peppers.

4 lbs. jalapeño peppers,
   thinly sliced
2 lbs. onion, thinly sliced
1/2 c. vinegar
1/2 c. water
6 c. sugar
2 T. mustard seed

2 t. turmeric
1 t. ground ginger
1 T. garlic powder
Optional: 2 t. celery seed
7 1-pint canning jars
   and lids, sterilized

Combine peppers, onion, vinegar and water in a large saucepan. Bring to a boil over medium-high heat. Reduce heat; simmer until tender, about 10 minutes. Drain, leaving a small amount of vinegar mixture in saucepan. Stir in sugar and spices. Cook until mixture reaches the soft-ball stage, or 234 to 240 degrees on a candy thermometer. Spoon into hot sterilized jars, leaving 1/4-inch headspace. Wipe rims; secure with lids and rings. Keep refrigerated. Makes about 7 jars.

Homespun is easy to fringe for table napkins, tablecloths and runners. Choose warm seasonal colors like brown, orange and amber.

Apple-Cinnamon Jelly

Kelly Alderson
Erie, PA

*Dissolve some red cinnamon candies
along with the sugar for beautiful red jelly.*

3 c. apple juice
2 T. lemon juice
5 c. sugar
2 t. cinnamon

1-3/4 oz. pkg. powdered pectin
3/4 c. water
6 1/2-pint freezer-safe plastic
     containers and lids, sterilized

Combine juices, sugar and cinnamon in a large bowl. Stir for several minutes until sugar is well dissolved; set aside. Combine pectin and water in a small saucepan over medium heat. Stir until mixture comes to a boil; boil for one minute. Add pectin mixture to apple juice mixture; stir until thoroughly mixed. Spoon into sterilized containers, leaving 1/2-inch headspace. Secure lids; let stand at room temperature for 24 hours, until set. May keep refrigerated for up to 3 months or frozen for up to one year. Makes 6 containers.

The tints of autumn...a mighty flower garden
blossoming under the spell of
the enchanter, frost.

-John Greenleaf Whittier

Gran's Pear Honey

Megan Brooks
Antioch, TN

Delicious on warm biscuits.

2 c. Anjou pears, cored,
  peeled and crushed
3 c. sugar
1/4 t. salt

1 lemon or orange, peeled
  and finely chopped
2 1-pint canning jars
  and lids, sterilized

Combine all ingredients in a heavy pan over low heat, stirring occasionally, for about 15 minutes, or until mixture reaches a spreading consistency. Pour into hot sterilized jars, leaving 1/4-inch headspace. Wipe rims; secure with lids and rings. Process in a boiling water bath for 15 minutes; set jars on a towel to cool. Check for seals. Makes about 2 jars.

Make a fun porch sign for Halloween...stencil a saying like
"Best Witches" or "Sit for a Spell" on an old plank.

Applecot Fruit Leather

Laura Fuller
Fort Wayne, IN

A healthy snack the kids will love...much better than store-bought!

24-oz. jar applesauce   1/2 t. cinnamon
10 dried apricots, chopped

Purée ingredients together in a blender. Pour into a 13"x9" baking pan that has been sprayed with non-stick vegetable spray. Shake pan gently from side to side until evenly distributed. Bake at 150 degrees for 5 to 7 hours, until flexible and no longer sticky. Cool in pan; cut into strips. Roll up each strip in plastic wrap; store in a covered container. Makes about 1-1/2 dozen pieces.

When tidying up the garden before winter, save clippings from herb plants like rosemary, thyme and lavender. Tossed into a fire in the fireplace, they'll give off an aromatic scent.

Overnight Apple Butter

Patty Fosnight
Channelview, TX

Wouldn't your family & friends love a jar of this old-time spread?

8 apples, cored, peeled
   and chopped
4 c. sugar
5 t. cinnamon
1 t. ground ginger

1/4 t. ground cloves
1/4 t. salt
8   1/2-pint canning jars and lids,
   sterilized

Combine all ingredients in a slow cooker. Cover and cook on high setting for one hour. Reduce to low setting; cook for 12 hours, stirring occasionally, until thickened and dark golden. Spoon into hot sterilized jars, leaving 3/4-inch headspace. Wipe rims; secure with lids and rings. Process in a boiling water bath for 20 minutes; set on towels to cool. Check for seals. Makes 8 jars.

Tuck a jar of Overnight Apple Butter into a basket of fresh-baked muffins for a pick-me-up gift that anyone would appreciate.

Trail Jerky

Kelly Massman
Decatur, IN

Spicy and satisfying...tuck a few pieces in
your pocket for your next fall outing!

5 lbs. ground beef
9 T. salt
2 t. garlic salt
1-1/4 t. tender-quick salt
1 T. flavor enhancer
1 T. pepper

1-1/4 t. cardamom
1 t. red pepper flakes
1 t. dried marjoram
2 T. smoke-flavored
   cooking sauce
2 T. water

Mix ground beef, salts and spices together in a large bowl; roll out
to 1/4-inch thickness on ungreased baking sheets. Set aside.
Combine cooking sauce and water; brush some of mixture over beef.
Bake at 200 degrees or lowest oven temperature for 2 hours; turn
over. Brush with remaining sauce mixture; bake until done, about one
hour. Cut into strips with kitchen scissors or a pizza cutter. Store in an
airtight container; keep refrigerated. Makes 5 dozen pieces.

Sometimes the simplest front door decorations are the prettiest!
Gather 5 or 6 brightly colored ears of Indian corn by the
dried husks and tie with a big ribbon bow.

Kraut & Pickled Eggs

Elinor Wieczorek
San Antonio, TX

A zesty side for roasts or sandwiches.

1-1/2 doz. eggs, hard-boiled
   and peeled
14-oz. can sauerkraut,
   drained and rinsed
1 c. celery, chopped
1/2 c. onion, chopped

1 green pepper, chopped
1/4 c. carrot, peeled
   and shredded
1-oz. jar pimentos, drained
2-1/2 c. sugar
3/4 c. vinegar

Combine all ingredients except sugar and vinegar in a very large glass or plastic container; set aside. Stir together sugar and vinegar in a saucepan. Cook over medium-low heat until sugar dissolves; pour over ingredients in container. Cover; refrigerate for at least 12 hours before serving. Keep refrigerated. Makes 1-1/2 dozen eggs and about 4-1/2 cups kraut.

Visit a neighborhood garden center for fall fun...all-you-can-carry pumpkins, shiny gourds, corn shocks to decorate the porch posts and maybe even a cup of cool cider.

A harvest gift to share...

Have fun gathering the ingredients from woods, fields, the garden and even the kitchen.

Bake cleaned pumpkin seeds, squash seeds and nuts on baking sheets at 350 degrees for 10 minutes, until dry but not toasted. Dry fresh herbs on paper towel-covered trays until crisp. Indian corn and sunflower seeds will dry right on the plant.

Thanksgiving Potpourri

Michelle Campen
Peoria, IL

Add a drop or two of cinnamon essential oil for fragrance, if you like. Pack in pretty jars for gift giving.

2 c. hickory nuts
2 c. acorns
2 c. dried goldenrod
2 c. dried basil
1 c. dried Indian corn kernels
1 c. dried sage

1 c. dried lovage
1 c. evening primrose pods
1/2 c. sunflower seeds
1/2 c. pumpkin seeds
1/2 c. squash seeds

Mix all ingredients together; store in lidded glass jars.
Makes about 13 cups, enough for several jars.

We Gather
TOGETHER

Pot Roast & Sweet Potatoes

Barbara Schmeckpeper
Minooka, IL

*I love sweet potatoes and I'm always looking for new ways
to serve them...they have such a good flavor in this recipe.*

1-1/2 to 2-lb. boneless beef
    chuck roast
2 T. oil
1 onion, thinly sliced
3 sweet potatoes, peeled
    and quartered
2/3 c. beef broth

3/4 t. celery salt
1/4 t. salt
1/4 t. pepper
1/4 t. cinnamon
1 T. cornstarch
2 T. cold water

In a skillet, brown roast on all sides in hot oil; drain. Place onion and
sweet potatoes in a slow cooker; top with roast. Combine broth and
seasonings; pour over all. Cover and cook on low setting for 10 to
12 hours, or on high setting for 4 to 5 hours. Place roast on a serving
platter, surrounded with vegetables; keep warm. Combine cornstarch
and water in a small saucepan; add one cup of juices from slow
cooker. Cook and stir over medium heat until thickened and bubbly;
continue cooking and stirring an additional 2 minutes. Serve gravy
with roast. Serves 4.

For a quick & easy table runner, choose cotton fabric printed
with autumn leaves, Indian corn and pumpkins in glowing gold,
orange and brown. Simply pink the edges...it will dress up
the dinner table all season long!

We Gather
TOGETHER

Harvest Home Roast Turkey

Lynn Williams
Muncie, IN

Delicious, yet so easy to prepare!

14 to 15-lb. turkey, thawed
2 cloves garlic, halved and
    divided
1 t. seasoning salt, divided
1 onion, quartered

1 bunch fresh parsley
2 fresh thyme sprigs
5 to 6 leaves fresh sage
2 T. olive oil
pepper to taste

Rinse turkey and pat dry. Remove giblets and neck; reserve
for another use. Rub inside of turkey with one clove garlic and
1/2 teaspoon salt; stuff with remaining garlic, onion and herbs.
Place turkey breast-side up on a rack in a large roaster pan. Brush
oil over turkey; sprinkle with remaining salt and pepper to taste.
Roast turkey at 325 degrees about 2-3/4 to 3 hours, basting
occasionally with pan drippings, until a meat thermometer inserted
into thickest part of thigh registers 180 degrees. If needed, tent
turkey with aluminum foil to prevent browning too quickly. Let
turkey stand 15 to 20 minutes before carving; discard garlic,
onion and herbs. Makes 10 to 12 servings.

Forever on Thanksgiving Day
The heart will find the pathway home.

-Wilbur D. Nesbit

Apricot-Glazed Baked Ham

Debbie Donaldson
Florala, AL

I prefer a lower-sodium ham...with this glaze, it's just as full of flavor as a regular ham. Sometimes we use pineapple preserves instead.

1 T. all-purpose flour
6 to 7-lb. fully-cooked ham
18-oz. jar apricot preserves
1/4 c. spicy brown mustard
1 c. brown sugar, packed
1/2 c. orange juice

Shake flour in a large oven bag. Place ham in bag; set in a roaster pan. Combine remaining ingredients, mixing well; pour over ham. Close bag with nylon tie provided; cut 6 to 8 slits in bag. Bake at 325 degrees for 2 hours to 2 hours and 20 minutes, or until a meat thermometer inserted into thickest part of ham reads 140 degrees. Serves 10 to 15.

Dress up clear glass votives in a flash. Simply cut strips
of decorative paper to fit, wrap around votives and fasten
in place with a bit of clear tape.

Cranberry Chicken

Vickie Callis
Gwynn, VA

Serve with wild rice and steamed asparagus
for a simple yet festive meal.

2 T. oil
4 to 6 boneless, skinless
   chicken breasts
1 onion, sliced
1/2 c. catsup

8-oz. can whole-berry
   cranberry sauce
2 T. brown sugar, packed
1 T. Worcestershire sauce

Heat oil in a large skillet over medium heat; add chicken and cook until golden on both sides. Remove chicken to a lightly greased 13"x9" baking pan. Add onion to skillet; sauté until tender, about 3 to 5 minutes. Stir in remaining ingredients; heat through. Pour mixture over chicken; bake, uncovered, at 350 degrees for 20 to 25 minutes. Serves 4 to 6.

A big pumpkin carved with your house number will lead guests right to your door. Sketch numbers freehand or trace with a stencil, carve them out and slip a votive candle inside...aren't you clever!

Pizzeria Pot Pie

Susie Backus
Gooseberry Patch

Be creative...adjust ingredients to suit your own taste.
Use spicy Italian sausage instead of turkey, add some sliced
pepperoni and black olives. Your kids will love it!

1 lb. ground turkey sausage
1/2 c. onion, chopped
1-1/2 c. sliced mushrooms
1 c. green pepper, chopped
14-1/2 oz. can chunky
   pizza sauce

2 c. biscuit baking mix
1/4 c. milk
1 egg, beaten
2 T. grated Parmesan cheese

Brown sausage and onion in a skillet over medium heat; drain.
Stir in mushrooms, pepper and pizza sauce; spoon into an ungreased
3-quart casserole dish and set aside. Stir baking mix, milk, egg and
cheese together until dough forms. Turn onto a floured surface; knead
10 times. Pat into a 9-inch circle; cut into 6 wedges. Arrange wedges
over sauce mixture. Bake, uncovered, at 400 degrees for about
30 minutes, until crust is golden. Serves 6.

A simple country-style bouquet...
so sweet! Place smooth pebbles
in the bottom of a Mason jar,
fill with water and arrange
black-eyed Susans inside.
Top off with a raffia bow.

Chicken Cacciatore

Debbie Anderson
Lafayette, IN

*We love coming home from frosty fall fun to the aroma
of this hearty dinner simmering in the slow cooker.*

1 onion, thinly sliced
3 lbs. chicken
2 6-oz. cans tomato paste
4-oz. can sliced mushrooms,
    drained
1 t. salt

1 to 2 cloves garlic, minced
1 to 2 t. dried oregano
1/2 t. celery seed
1 bay leaf
1/2 c. water
cooked spaghetti

Place onion in a slow cooker; add chicken pieces. Stir together
remaining ingredients except spaghetti and pour over chicken. Cover
and cook on low setting for 7 to 9 hours, or on high setting for 3 to
4 hours. Discard bay leaf. Serve chicken and sauce over cooked
spaghetti. Serves 4 to 6.

The holidays are just around the corner...time to check your
spice rack! Crush a pinch of each spice. If it has a fresh, zingy
scent, it's still good. Toss out old-smelling spices and stock up
on any that you've used up during the year.

Hamburger Crunch

Gayle Ortmeyer
Jefferson City, MO

If you have any leftovers, roll them up in
flour tortillas for tasty burritos.

2 lbs. ground beef
1 T. onion, minced
2 10-3/4 oz. cans tomato soup
1 t. chili powder

4 c. corn chips, slightly crushed
8-oz. pkg. shredded Cheddar
   cheese

Brown ground beef and onion together in a large skillet over
medium heat; drain. Stir in soup and chili powder. Spread in an
ungreased 13"x9" baking pan; top with corn chips. Bake, uncovered,
at 350 degrees for 20 to 25 minutes. Remove from oven; sprinkle
with cheese. Bake for an additional 5 minutes. Serves 6 to 8.

Thanksgiving Day is a fine time to catch up on the past year
with family & friends. Set up a family memory table and have
everybody bring along snapshots, clippings, even Junior's
baseball trophy and Aunt Sue's latest knitting project...
you'll all have so much to talk about together!

Speedy Spaghetti Supper

Audrey Lett
Newark, DE

Pop some garlic bread in the oven...
dinner will be ready before you know it!

1/2 lb. Italian pork sausage,
   sliced
1/2 lb. ground beef
1 c. green pepper, chopped
8-oz. pkg. spaghetti, uncooked
   and broken into thirds

26-oz. jar favorite-flavor
   spaghetti sauce
2 c. water
Garnish: grated Parmesan
   cheese

Brown sausage in a skillet over medium-high heat; add beef. Cook,
stirring occasionally, until beef is browned; drain. Add green pepper,
uncooked spaghetti, sauce and water; bring to a boil. Reduce heat;
cover and simmer for 14 to 16 minutes, or until spaghetti is tender.
Sprinkle with Parmesan cheese. Serves 4 to 6.

Collect autumn leaves to use as coasters for a burst of color on the
dinner table. Write guests' names along the edge with a gold or
copper paint pen...they'll double as placecards too.

German Sauerbraten

Karin Duemmlein
Saratoga, CA

*Real old-country flavor! The roast is marinated for
several days before baking, and it's worth it.*

4-lb. beef eye of round
   or rump roast
2 onions, sliced
1-1/2 c. water
1-1/2 c. red wine vinegar
1 T. sugar
1 T. salt

12 whole cloves
6 bay leaves
6 peppercorns
1/4 t. ground ginger
1 to 2 T. oil
5 carrots, peeled and halved
1 to 2 c. water

Place roast in an ungreased 13"x9" glass baking pan; set aside.
Combine remaining ingredients except oil, carrots and water; pour
over roast. Cover and refrigerate for 4 to 5 days, turning twice daily.
Remove roast from pan; discard marinade. Heat oil over medium heat
in a large skillet; brown roast on all sides. Place roast in a roaster pan;
add carrots and water to pan. Cover and bake at 325 degrees for
3 hours, until roast is very tender. Serve with gravy from roaster.
Serves 4 to 6.

To God who gives our daily bread
A thankful song we raise,
And pray that he who sends us food
May fill our hearts with praise.

-Thomas Tallis

Easy Brunswick Stew

Denise Neal
Castle Rock, CO

*This is one of my family's favorite cool-weather meals...
it's fast and very yummy! You can even save time by
using precooked chicken and bacon.*

1/2 c. onion, diced
1 T. oil
3 slices bacon, crisply cooked
   and crumbled
2 14-1/2 oz. cans chicken broth
8-oz. can tomato sauce

2 c. potatoes, peeled and cubed
1 c. lima or kidney beans
1 c. frozen corn
3 c. cooked chicken breast, diced
salt and pepper to taste

In a large stockpot over medium heat, sauté onion in oil until tender.
Add bacon, broth, sauce and vegetables; bring to a boil over high heat.
Reduce heat to a simmer; cook for 30 minutes. Stir in chicken, salt and
pepper; heat through. Serves 6.

Serve tummy-warming stews in edible mini pumpkins just for fun!
Cut tops off pumpkins, scoop out seeds and brush lightly with oil.
Bake on a baking sheet at 350 degrees for 30 to 40 minutes,
until tender. Ladle in hot stew...yum!

Garlic & Lemon Roasted Chicken

Terry Esposito
Freehold, NJ

This is one of my favorite recipes. It smells wonderful as it's cooking and tastes delicious too...fit for Sunday dinner.

4-lb. roasting chicken
1 lemon, halved
1/2 t. salt
1/2 t. pepper
1/2 t. dried parsley
7 cloves garlic, divided

1/4 c. butter, softened
  and divided
3 T. water
1 lb. potatoes, peeled and cubed
2 c. baby carrots

Place chicken in a lightly greased 13"x9" roasting pan. Squeeze lemon over chicken; place lemon halves inside chicken. Sprinkle salt, pepper and parsley over chicken inside and out. Press one to 2 cloves garlic through a garlic press; rub over chicken. Halve remaining cloves garlic and stuff inside chicken. Rub one tablespoon butter over chicken; place remaining butter inside chicken. Pour water into pan. Cover tightly with aluminum foil, making sure foil doesn't touch top of chicken. Bake at 375 degrees for 20 minutes. Add potatoes and carrots to pan; cover again. Bake for an additional 40 minutes to one hour, until juices run clear, basting occasionally with pan juices. Serves 4 to 6.

Start a new tradition for Thanksgiving...decorate a blank book and invite guests to write what they're thankful for. The book will become even more meaningful as it's continued year to year.

We Gather
TOGETHER

One-Pot Chicken & Noodles

Elizabeth Blackstone
Racine, WI

Pure comfort food!

26-oz. can cream of chicken
    soup
10-3/4 oz. can cream of
    mushroom soup
3 14-1/2 oz. cans chicken broth
2 c. cooked chicken breast, diced

2 t. onion powder
1 t. seasoning salt
1/2 t. garlic powder
2 9-oz. pkgs. frozen wide
    egg noodles

Combine soups, broth and chicken in a large pot; bring to a boil over medium-high heat. Add remaining ingredients; reduce heat to low and simmer for 20 to 30 minutes, until noodles are tender. Serves 6.

For a quick fall centerpiece, set a spicy-scented
orange pillar candle in a shallow dish. Surround
with unshelled hazelnuts or acorns...done!

Skillet Dinner

Denise Oravecz
Pittsburgh, PA

Hearty and filling!

1 lb. ground beef
1 onion, chopped
1 green pepper, chopped
14-1/2 oz. can beef broth
2/3 c. water

1 c. long-cooking rice, uncooked
1/2 t. dry mustard
1 tomato, chopped
1 c. shredded Pepper Jack cheese

Brown ground beef and onion in a large skillet over medium heat; drain. Stir in green pepper, broth, water, rice and dry mustard; bring to a boil. Reduce heat; simmer until liquid is absorbed, about 25 minutes. Stir in tomato; sprinkle cheese over top. Cover and remove from heat. Let stand for 2 to 3 minutes, until cheese melts. Serves 4 to 6.

Cute placecards...so easy the kids can make them! Curl colorful chenille stems around pencils, then around the stems of mini gourds. Slide placecards between the curls and set one at each place.

We Gather
TOGETHER

Hallie's Skillet Dried Beef & Corn

Emily Johnson
Lyons, IN

My sister Hallie gave me this recipe years ago. She's no longer with us, but she looks over my shoulder each time I fix this meal.

2-1/2 oz. jar dried beef, chopped
2 T. onion, finely chopped
1 t. butter
1 T. all-purpose flour
3/4 c. milk

15-oz. can creamed corn
2 T. green pepper, diced
3/4 c. shredded sharp
  Cheddar cheese
toast slices or cornbread squares

Sauté dried beef and onion in butter over medium heat until beef begins to curl; stir in flour, mixing well. Add milk; cook until thickened. Add corn and heat through. Stir in green pepper and cheese; cook over low heat until cheese melts. Spoon over toast or cornbread to serve. Serves 4.

Add an extra can or 2 of soup, veggies or tuna
to the grocery cart every week, then put aside these
extras at home. Before you know it, you'll have a
generous selection of canned goods for fall food drives.

Savory Turkey Loaf

Kim Hill-DeGroot
Macomb Township, MI

Not your ordinary meatloaf! Grated apple helps keep it moist.

1 t. oil
1 c. onion, chopped
1 stalk celery, chopped
3/4 t. dried thyme
1/2 t. dried sage
1-1/2 lbs. ground turkey
1-1/2 c. bread crumbs

1-1/2 c. apple, cored, peeled
   and grated
1 egg, beaten
2 T. fresh parsley, chopped
1 T. mustard
3/4 t. salt
1/2 t. pepper

Heat oil in a skillet; add onion and celery. Sauté for about 3 minutes; stir in thyme and sage. Cool slightly; combine mixture with remaining ingredients in a bowl and mix well. Shape into a loaf; place in a greased 8"x4" loaf pan. Bake, uncovered, at 350 degrees for one hour. Drain drippings from pan; brush glaze over top of loaf. Return to oven; bake until top is golden, about 10 to 15 minutes. Serves 6 to 8.

Glaze:

2 T. cider vinegar
2 T. brown sugar, packed

2 t. mustard

Stir ingredients together in a bowl until brown sugar dissolves.

Thanksgiving is so family-centered...why not have a post-holiday potluck with friends, the weekend after Turkey Day? Everyone can bring their favorite "leftover" concoctions and relax together.

Turkey-Almond Casserole

Janet Allen
Dalton Gardens, ID

*Even my husband likes this scrumptious dish, and he's a real meat
& potatoes man! It's the best use for leftover turkey I've found.*

2 10-3/4 oz. cans cream of
    mushroom soup
1/2 c. mayonnaise
1/2 c. sour cream
2 T. onion, chopped
2 T. lemon juice
1 t. salt
1/2 t. pepper
5 c. cooked turkey, cubed

3 c. cooked rice
4 stalks celery, chopped
8-oz. can sliced water chestnuts,
    drained
1-1/4 c. sliced almonds, divided
1-1/2 c. round buttery cracker
    crumbs
1/3 c. butter, melted

Combine soup, mayonnaise, sour cream, onion, lemon juice, salt
and pepper in a large bowl; mix well. Stir in turkey, rice, celery,
water chestnuts and one cup almonds. Transfer to a greased
13"x9" baking pan; set aside. Mix remaining almonds, cracker crumbs
and butter; sprinkle over top. Bake, uncovered, at 350 degrees for
35 to 40 minutes, until bubbly and golden. Serves 6.

Purchase a bundle of wheat straw at a craft store.
Arrange a few stalks on each folded napkin for a
beautiful yet simple reminder of a bountiful harvest.

Pork Chops with Apple Stuffing

Sherry Noble
Kennett, MO

A cozy meal to share with friends.

1 T. olive oil
3 T. butter, divided
5 boneless pork chops
1 apple, cored and chopped

1/2 c. onion, chopped
1-2/3 c. water
6-oz. pkg. stuffing mix

Heat oil and one tablespoon butter in a large non-stick skillet over medium heat. Add pork chops; cook for 8 to 10 minutes, turning once. Remove chops; cover to keep warm. Melt remaining butter in skillet; add apple and onion. Cook for 3 to 5 minutes, stirring occasionally, until tender. Add water; bring to a boil. Stir in stuffing mix; remove from heat. Arrange chops over stuffing mixture; cover and let stand for 5 minutes before serving. Serves 5.

Invert a glass garden cloche and fill it with mini gourds, nuts and interesting seed pods. Top with a tray and turn right-side up for a pretty display on a mantel or sideboard.

Rosemary Chicken & Tomatoes
Vickie

Tender, slow-simmered chicken at its best.

1 T. oil
2 lbs. skinless chicken thighs
2/3 c. chicken broth
1/4 c. white wine or
    chicken broth
2 cloves garlic, minced
salt and pepper to taste

6 plum tomatoes, chopped
2 green peppers, cut into strips
1-1/2 c. sliced mushrooms
2 T. cornstarch
2 T. cold water
2 t. fresh rosemary, snipped
cooked egg noodles or rice

Heat oil in a skillet over medium heat. Sauté chicken until golden, about 5 minutes. Drain. Add broth, wine or broth, garlic, salt and pepper to skillet; bring to a boil. Reduce heat; cover and simmer for about 20 minutes. Add tomatoes, peppers and mushrooms. Simmer, covered, for 15 minutes, until chicken is cooked through. Transfer chicken to a serving dish; cover to keep warm. In a small bowl, combine cornstarch, water and rosemary; stir into vegetable mixture. Cook and stir until thickened and bubbly; cook for an additional 2 minutes. Serve chicken over noodles or rice; spoon sauce over chicken. Serves 5.

Younger guests will feel oh-so grown up when you serve them bubbly sparkling cider in long-stemmed plastic glasses.

Old-Fashioned Beef Stew

Robin Guyor
Berkley, MI

This is a fall favorite for my family. Served over buttery biscuits,
it's a perfect comfort food for any day.

1 lb. stew beef, cut into
    1/2-inch cubes
2 T. all-purpose flour
2 t. oil
1 yellow onion, thinly sliced
2 c. sliced mushrooms
2 cloves garlic, minced
6 T. tomato paste
2 c. beef broth

2 c. carrots, peeled and
    thinly sliced
2 potatoes, peeled and diced
1 c. green beans
1/4 c. fresh parsley, chopped
1 T. cornstarch
1 T. cold water
Optional: additional fresh
    parsley, chopped

Toss beef with flour, shaking off excess; set aside. Heat oil over
medium heat in a large stockpot. Sauté beef over medium heat until
browned on all sides, about 6 minutes. Push beef to one side of
stockpot. Add onion and mushrooms; sauté for about 6 minutes. Stir
in garlic; sauté for one additional minute. Stir in tomato paste and
broth. Add vegetables and parsley; add enough water to just cover.
Bring to a boil; reduce heat to low and simmer until beef is tender,
about 2 hours. Combine cornstarch and water in a small bowl; stir into
stew and simmer for an additional 30 minutes. Sprinkle with
additional parsley, if desired. Serves 4 to 6.

Gather pine cones and brush lightly
with craft glue, then sprinkle with
clear glitter...sparkly heaped in a
wooden bowl and oh-so easy!

Mom's Cassoulet

Jennifer Denny
Delaware, OH

*Mmm…the flavors of the sausage, ham and beans
slowly blend together as they cook.*

1/2 lb. Italian pork sausage,
   cooked and diced
1/2 lb. cooked ham, cubed
2 16-oz. cans navy beans
8-oz. can tomato sauce
1/4 c. catsup

1/4 c. water
1 onion, diced
2 T. brown sugar, packed
1/2 t. dry mustard
1/2 t. salt
1/4 t. pepper

Combine all ingredients in an ungreased 13"x9" baking pan;
bake at 350 degrees for one hour. Serves 4 to 6.

Two sounds of autumn are unmistakable…the hurrying
rustle of crisp leaves blown along the street…by a gusty wind,
and the gabble of a flock of migrating geese.

-Hal Borland

Oven-Fried Pecan Chicken

Connie Bryant
Topeka, KS

Absolutely delicious fresh from the oven! Or chill, then wrap individual pieces in wax paper for a fall picnic.

1/2 c. all-purpose flour
1 t. salt
3/4 t. pepper
1 t. paprika
1/2 t. dried oregano
1/2 t. ground cumin

1/8 t. cayenne pepper
3/4 c. buttermilk
2 c. pecans, finely ground
1/2 c. corn flake cereal, crushed
5 T. butter, melted
4 lbs. chicken

Combine flour and seasonings in a shallow dish; pour buttermilk into another shallow dish. Combine pecans and cereal in a third shallow dish; set aside. Spread butter in a 15"x10" jelly-roll pan. Dip chicken pieces first into flour mixture, then into buttermilk; let drain slightly, then dip into pecan mixture, turning to coat well; arrange in jelly-roll pan. Bake, uncovered, at 400 degrees for about 50 minutes, until chicken is golden, crisp and tender, turning once after 25 minutes. Drain on paper towels; serve warm or cold. Makes 6 to 8 servings.

Dinner:
Roast Turkey
Mashed Potatoes
Apple Crisp

Show off the Thanksgiving menu in a rustic frame.
Select several straight twigs and tie together at the corners
with jute. Decorate the corners with tiny acorns.

Joyful Quilters' Chicken Casserole

Tracy Wright
Dripping Springs, TX

*Several ladies in my church get together to quilt, craft and visit.
When we went on a quilters' weekend retreat, one of the ladies shared
this dish. It was an instant hit...a true "pattern" for success!*

2 c. onion, chopped
2 T. butter
10-oz. pkg. baby spinach
10-3/4 oz. can cream of chicken
  soup
2/3 c. cream of mushroom soup
2 T. chopped green chiles
10-oz. can tomatoes with chiles

1 c. sour cream
1-1/2 t. salt
12-oz. pkg. tortilla chips, divided
4 to 6 c. cooked chicken breasts,
  chopped and divided
8-oz. pkg. shredded Monterey
  Jack cheese, divided

Sauté onion in butter in a large skillet over medium heat. Stir in
spinach, soups, chiles, tomatoes with chiles, sour cream and salt. In a
lightly greased 13"x9" baking pan, alternate layers of chips, chicken,
spinach mixture and cheese. Repeat layers, ending with cheese. Bake,
uncovered, at 350 degrees for 30 to 40 minutes, until lightly golden
on top. Let stand for 5 minutes before serving. Serves 8 to 10.

For placecards that are oh-so-sweet, have the kids trace
around their hands on construction paper, then color with
crayons to create turkeys. Grandma will love it!

Lasagna Toss

Jana Warnell
Kalispell, MT

Lasagna for dinner…quick & easy! Use bowtie pasta or rotini
if your grocer doesn't have the mini lasagna.

1/2 lb. ground beef
1/2 lb. ground Italian pork
   sausage
1/2 c. onion, chopped
1/2 t. salt

1/8 t. garlic powder
1-3/4 c. spaghetti sauce
6-oz. pkg. mini lasagna, cooked
1 c. cottage cheese
2 c. shredded mozzarella cheese

Brown together ground beef, sausage, onion, salt and garlic powder
in a large skillet; drain. Stir in sauce; simmer until heated through.
Stir in mini lasagna and cottage cheese. Spoon into a lightly greased
2-quart casserole dish; top with mozzarella cheese. Bake, uncovered,
at 350 degrees for 20 to 25 minutes. Serves 6.

Encourage table talk among dinner guests who don't
know each other well...just write each person's
name on both sides of his or her placecard,
where other guests can see it!

Pesto Baked Pasta

Susie Purvis
San Diego, CA

This dish can be prepared 2 days ahead. Just cover and refrigerate...remove from fridge 30 minutes before baking.

1 lb. sweet Italian ground
   pork sausage
1 sweet onion, finely chopped
4 cloves garlic, minced
4 c. marinara sauce
6 T. basil pesto sauce
salt and pepper to taste

16-oz. pkg. penne pasta, cooked
8-oz. pkg. mozzarella cheese,
   finely diced
1 c. shredded Parmesan cheese,
   divided
6-oz. pkg. baby spinach

In a skillet over medium heat, brown sausage for 5 minutes. Add onion; sauté until tender. Stir in garlic; cook for one minute. Drain; add sauce and simmer until sauce begins to thicken, about 10 minutes. Stir in pesto, salt and pepper; remove from heat. Spread a thin layer of sauce mixture in a lightly greased 13"x9" baking pan. Combine remaining sauce mixture with pasta, mozzarella cheese, half the Parmesan cheese and spinach; mix well. Spoon into baking pan; sprinkle with remaining Parmesan cheese. Bake, uncovered, at 375 degrees for about 30 minutes, until golden and bubbly. Makes 6 to 8 servings.

Pressed autumn leaves look colorful scattered on a crisp white tablecloth. Layer leaves between paper towels, then between sections of newspaper. Top with a heavy book or other weight...leaves will be ready in a week or 2.

Garlic Swiss Steak

Jacqueline Kurtz
Reading, PA

Just like Grandma used to make...serve with mashed potatoes.

1/3 c. all-purpose flour	2 T. oil
1 t. salt	14-oz. can stewed tomatoes
1/2 t. pepper	1/2 c. onion, chopped
1-1/2 lbs. beef round steak, cut into serving-size portions	1/2 green pepper, chopped
	2 cloves garlic, minced

Combine flour, salt and pepper; sprinkle over steak and pound into both sides. In a large skillet, brown steak in oil over medium heat; transfer to a lightly greased 13"x9" baking pan. Combine remaining ingredients; pour over steak. Cover and bake at 350 degrees for one to 1-1/2 hours, or until tender. Makes 6 servings.

Set the table for Thanksgiving with a plain white cloth.
Have everyone sign and date it with a permanent marker or,
if you're crafty, in pencil to embroider later. Small children can
trace their handprints. Next year, repeat...a new tradition!

We Gather
TOGETHER

Slow-Cooked Teriyaki Pork Roast

Jodi Erdmann
Watertown, WI

*For another tasty meal, shred the cooked pork and stir
it into the hot gravy, then spoon onto toasted buns.*

3/4 c. apple juice
2 T. sugar
2 T. soy sauce
1 T. cider vinegar
1 t. ground ginger
1/4 t. garlic powder

1/8 t. pepper
2 to 3-lb. boneless center-cut
    rolled pork roast
1-1/2 T. cornstarch
3 T. cold water

Combine first 7 ingredients in a slow cooker; mix well. Add roast,
turning to coat; place roast fat-side up. Cover and cook on low setting
for 7 to 8 hours, or on high setting for 3 to 4 hours. Strain liquid into
a small saucepan; bring to a boil. Mix together cornstarch and water
in a small bowl; add to boiling liquid. Cook until thickened. Slice roast,
serving gravy over top. Serves 4 to 6.

Hard-shelled fall squash can be difficult to cut for cooking. Do it the
easy way, in the microwave! Cook the whole squash on high setting for
5 minutes, pierce with a knife tip to check for tenderness and cook a few
more minutes as needed. Cool, cut in half and scoop out seeds...simple!

Farmhouse Pork & Cabbage Sauté

Jo Ann

A hearty, warming one-dish dinner.

4 thick pork loin chops
3/4 t. salt, divided
1/4 t. pepper, divided
6 slices bacon, crisply cooked,
    crumbled and drippings
    reserved
1 t. olive oil
1 onion, thinly sliced

16-oz. pkg. shredded
    coleslaw mix
2 Golden Delicious apples,
    cored and sliced
3/4 lb. redskin potatoes, cubed
3/4 c. apple cider
1/4 t. dried thyme
1 T. cider vinegar

Sprinkle chops with 1/4 teaspoon salt and 1/8 teaspoon pepper; set aside. Heat reserved drippings and oil in a Dutch oven over medium-high heat. Cook chops until golden on both sides and nearly done, about 8 minutes. Remove chops to a plate; keep warm. Add onion to pan. Cover and cook over medium heat for 8 to 10 minutes, stirring occasionally, until tender and golden. Gradually stir in coleslaw; cook until wilted, about 5 minutes. Add apples, potatoes, cider, thyme and remaining salt and pepper; bring to a boil. Reduce heat; cover and simmer for 15 minutes, until potatoes are tender. Stir in vinegar; return chops to pan and heat through. Garnish with reserved bacon. Makes 4 servings.

Arrange shiny fresh fruits and vegetables in a wicker
cornucopia for a tried & true centerpiece.

Maple-Curry Pork Roast

Sharon Demers
Dolores, CO

This is wonderful on a cool fall day served with oven-roasted root vegetables, homemade applesauce and sweet potato biscuits.

1-1/2 lb. pork tenderloin
1/2 c. maple syrup
2 T. soy sauce
2 T. catsup
1 T. Dijon mustard

1-1/2 t. curry powder
1-1/2 t. ground coriander
1 t. Worcestershire sauce
2 cloves garlic, minced

Place roast in a large, heavy-duty plastic zipping bag; set aside. Whisk together remaining ingredients in a medium bowl. Pour over roast; refrigerate for at least one hour. Transfer roast with marinade to an ungreased 13"x9" baking pan; bake, uncovered, at 350 degrees for 40 minutes. Let roast stand for 10 minutes; slice thinly and drizzle with sauce from pan. Serves 6.

Wrap silverware in lengths of raffia, ribbon or homespun...
pretty enough for any harvest table.

Rosina's E-Z Chicken Skillet

Rosina Carter
Bay Saint Louis, MS

This is a very accommodating recipe. Add a little more macaroni, onion and pepper to feed extra guests, or use Mexican-seasoned tomatoes and serve over rice for a whole new dish.

1 T. oil
1/2 c. onion, diced
1/2 green pepper, diced
2 c. cooked chicken, diced
2 c. cooked elbow macaroni

15.8-oz. can Great Northern
    beans, drained and rinsed
14-1/2 oz. can Italian-seasoned
    diced tomatoes

Heat oil in a large skillet over medium heat. Add onion and green pepper; cook until tender. Stir in remaining ingredients; simmer until heated through, 15 to 20 minutes. Serves 4.

Give favorite pasta recipes a twist for fall...
pick up some pasta in seasonal shapes like
autumn leaves, pumpkins or turkeys! Some even
come in veggie colors like orange, red or green.

We Gather
TOGETHER

Hearty Ham & Rice Bake

Terees Grippe
Mukilteo, WA

This casserole is my "old reliable" when I want my family
& friends to have a full tummy and a big smile!

2 10-3/4 oz. cans cream of
   celery soup
1 c. light cream
1 c. shredded sharp Cheddar
   cheese
1/3 c. grated Parmesan cheese
1-1/2 T. onion, grated
1 T. mustard

1 t. lemon zest
1/4 t. dried rosemary
1/3 t. pepper
4 c. cooked rice
4 c. cooked ham, cubed
16-oz. can green beans, drained
6-oz. can French fried
   onion rings

Combine soup and cream in a large bowl; stir in cheeses, onion and
seasonings. Add rice, ham and beans; turn into a lightly greased
3-quart casserole dish. Sprinkle with onion rings. Bake, uncovered, at
350 degrees for one hour. Serves 10.

On a sunny autumn morn, take your coffee out to the front
porch...enjoy nature's beauty and wave to neighbors passing by!

Fireside Chili Pot

Sue Neely
Greenville, IL

Warms you down to your toes.

2 15-1/2 oz. cans chili with
   beans
2 c. cooked rice
1/2 c. onion, chopped

1/2 c. green pepper, chopped
1/4 c. sliced black olives
1/2 c. shredded Cheddar cheese

Mix together chili, rice, onion and green pepper in a large saucepan.
Heat over medium heat, stirring occasionally, for 20 minutes, until
bubbly. Sprinkle with olives and cheese; continue to cook until cheese
melts, about 5 minutes. Serves 6.

Hearty Chili Pie

Holly Sutton
Grahamsville, NY

A tasty way to enjoy extra homemade chili too...
just measure out about 4 cups chili.

4 15-oz. cans chili
2 7-oz. pkgs. cornbread mix

16-oz. pkg. shredded Cheddar
   cheese

Spread chili in a greased 13"x9" baking pan; set aside. Prepare
cornbread mix according to package directions; spoon batter over
chili. Bake at 350 degrees for 30 minutes, until cornbread is golden.
Sprinkle with cheese. Serves 6.

We Gather
TOGETHER

Aubrey's Favorite Beefy Stroganoff *Ursula Juarez-Wall*
Dumfries, VA

A great "Mom, we're hungry now!" recipe...
I rarely have any leftovers.

2 lbs. ground beef, browned
   and drained
2 10-3/4 oz. cans cream of
   mushroom soup
10-3/4 oz. can French onion
   soup
2/3 to 1 c. water

1/8 t. nutmeg
salt and pepper to taste
Optional: 4-oz. can sliced
   mushrooms, drained
8-oz. container sour cream
cooked wide egg noodles

In a large skillet, combine ground beef, soups, water, seasonings and mushrooms, if using. Simmer over medium heat for about 10 minutes. Just before serving, stir in sour cream and heat through. Serve over wide noodles. Serves 8 to 10.

Press whole cloves into a pillar candle
to create a pattern...simple!

Sharing recipe traditions...

Thanksgiving is the perfect time to collect everyone's tried & true recipes into a family recipe book!

Gather together...handwritten recipe cards like Grandma's Stuffing and Mary's Pumpkin Pie, copies from favorite old cookbooks and even recipes clipped from labels.

Be sure to include notes with the recipes..."I only use real butter for this!" Add funny stories too..."Remember the year that the dog ran off with the roast turkey?"

Photocopy the recipes...years from now, it will be sweet to read recipes in everyone's own handwriting. Assemble recipes into booklets with staples or pretty ribbons.

Crafty family members might enjoy scrapbooking...with snapshots, decorative papers and add-ons.

Make enough copies for everyone...family friends will want one too!

Seasonal SWEETS

No-Bake Maple-Peanut Drops

Mary Patenaude
Griswold, CT

A yummy variation on those old standbys, chocolate no-bake cookies.

1-1/2 c. sugar
1/2 c. milk
1/4 c. maple-flavored syrup
1/2 c. creamy peanut butter

2 t. vanilla extract
2 c. quick-cooking oats,
  uncooked

Combine sugar, milk and syrup in a medium saucepan; bring to a
rolling boil over medium heat, stirring frequently. Boil for 3 minutes;
stir in peanut butter and vanilla. Add oats, mixing well. Drop by
rounded teaspoonfuls onto wax paper. Cool for 3 to 4 hours until firm.
Makes about 2-1/2 dozen.

Add some pizazz to plain sugar cookies. Simply stir
some sunflower kernels or chopped dried fruit
into the dough before baking...yummy!

Diana's Apple Crisp Cookies

Diana Decker
Kerhonkson, NY

This makes a large batch of cookies, but they go so fast that it's worth the effort. They're always a big hit with everyone!

1-1/2 c. margarine, softened
1-1/2 c. dark brown sugar, packed
1 c. sugar
.7-oz. pkg. spiced apple drink mix
1 T. cinnamon
1-1/2 t. baking powder
1-1/2 t. baking soda
1/2 t. salt
3 eggs, beaten
2 t. vanilla extract
3 c. all-purpose flour
3 c. long-cooking oats, uncooked
1-1/2 c. raisins
1-1/2 c. dried apples, chopped
1 c. chopped walnuts

In a very large bowl, combine margarine, sugars, drink mix, cinnamon, baking powder, baking soda and salt. Mix well; blend in eggs and vanilla. Blend in as much of the flour as possible; stir in remaining ingredients. Drop by rounded teaspoonfuls onto ungreased baking sheets. Bake at 350 degrees for 10 to 12 minutes, or until light golden. Makes about 7 dozen.

Make short work of chopping nuts...seal them in a
plastic zipping bag and roll with a rolling pin.
No muss, no fuss!

Peanut Butter Apple Crisp

Linda Nichols
Wintersville, OH

Scrumptious served warm, topped with scoops of ice cream.

1 c. all-purpose flour
1-1/2 c. brown sugar, packed
1 t. cinnamon
3/4 c. creamy peanut butter
1/3 c. butter

6 to 8 tart apples, cored,
    peeled and thinly sliced
2 T. lemon juice
1 t. lemon zest

Combine flour, brown sugar and cinnamon in a medium bowl. Cut in peanut butter and butter until mixture resembles coarse crumbs; set aside. Arrange apple slices in a lightly greased 13"x9" baking pan; sprinkle with lemon juice and zest. Top apples with crumb mixture; bake at 350 degrees for 35 to 45 minutes. Serves 10 to 12.

Pick up some shiny new paint cans from the paint store to decorate. Fill them with baked goods to send home with guests. Later, the kids can use them as trick-or-treat pails!

Thanksgiving Pumpkin Pie Crunch

Karen Pilcher
Burleson, TX

Oh-so-easy...perfect for a Thanksgiving buffet.

15-oz. can pumpkin
12-oz. can evaporated milk
3 eggs, beaten
1-1/2 c. sugar
4 t. pumpkin pie spice
1/2 t. salt
18-1/2 oz. pkg. yellow cake mix
1 c. chopped pecans
1 c. butter, melted
Garnish: whipped topping

Combine pumpkin, evaporated milk, eggs, sugar, spice and salt in a large bowl. Beat with an electric mixer on low speed until well blended. Pour into a greased 13"x9" baking pan. Sprinkle with cake mix; top with pecans and drizzle with butter. Bake at 350 degrees for 50 to 55 minutes, until golden. Cool completely. Cut into squares; dollop with whipped topping. Refrigerate any leftovers. Serves 16.

Plump up dried cranberries and raisins for baking...
they'll be soft and tasty. Cover them with boiling water
and let stand about 15 minutes, then drain well and pat dry.

Pumpkin Caramel Flan

Rhonda Reeder
Ellicott City, MD

A deliciously different ending to a holiday meal.

3/4 c. sugar
2 eggs
2 egg whites
1 c. canned pumpkin
12-oz. can evaporated milk

1/2 c. honey
1-1/2 t. pumpkin pie spice
1 t. vanilla extract
1/2 t. salt

Set an ungreased 8"x8" baking pan in an ungreased 13"x9" baking pan; pour 3/4 inch of water into larger pan and set aside. Pour sugar into a saucepan; cook and stir over medium heat until melted and golden. Carefully pour into prepared 8"x8" pan; lift pan from water. Working quickly, swirl melted sugar around bottom and sides of pan. Return pan to water in 13"x9" pan; set aside. Beat together eggs and egg whites in a medium bowl. Add remaining ingredients; mix well and pour into 8"x8" pan. Bake at 350 degrees for 40 to 45 minutes, until set and the tip of a knife tests clean. Remove pan from water; cool on wire rack. Chill for 4 hours or overnight. To serve, run a small spatula around edge of flan. Holding a plate over pan, invert and shake gently to release. Cut in quarters diagonally; cut each quarter in half to form triangles. Top each serving with a spoonful of caramelized sauce from pan. Makes 8 servings.

Happiness being a dessert so sweet
May life give you more than you can ever eat.

-Irish Toast

Cinnamon Rice Pudding

Staci Meyers
Ideal, GA

*Dollop with whipped cream and top with a cherry,
just like Mom used to do.*

1 c. jasmine rice, uncooked
3 c. milk
1/2 c. sugar

4-inch cinnamon stick
1 t. vanilla extract
1/2 c. whipping cream, whipped

Cook rice according to package directions; stir in milk, sugar and cinnamon stick. Bring to a boil, uncovered, over medium heat. Reduce heat and simmer, for about 15 to 20 minutes, until thick and creamy, stirring occasionally. Discard cinnamon stick; cool. Stir in vanilla; gently fold in whipped cream. Serve warm or chilled. Makes 4 to 6.

Tuck an orange pillar candle into a hurricane and set it
on a wooden tray. Heap dried gourds and pine cones around it...
delightful on a sideboard.

Patti's Harvest Loaf Cake

Patti Blake
Grayling, MI

Packed with pumpkin, spices, chocolate, walnuts...yum!

1/2 c. butter
1 c. sugar
2 eggs
1-1/2 c. all-purpose flour
1 t. baking soda
1/2 t. salt
1 t. cinnamon

1/2 t. nutmeg
1/4 t. ground ginger
1/4 t. ground cloves
3/4 c. canned pumpkin
6-oz. pkg. semi-sweet
   chocolate chips
1 c. chopped walnuts, divided

Blend butter, sugar and eggs, beating well; set aside. Stir together flour, baking soda, salt and spices. Add to butter mixture alternately with pumpkin, beginning and ending with dry ingredients, beating well after each addition. Stir in chocolate chips and 3/4 cup walnuts. Pour into a greased 9"x5" loaf pan; sprinkle with remaining nuts. Bake at 350 degrees for 65 minutes, or until done. Drizzle Powdered Sugar Glaze over cooled cake. Makes 10 to 12 servings.

Powdered Sugar Glaze:

1/2 c. powdered sugar
2 T. light cream

1/8 t. cinnamon
1/8 t. nutmeg

Stir all ingredients together to a drizzling consistency.

Whenever you bake favorite cookies, fruit breads and pies, make a double batch to freeze. By the time the holidays arrive, you'll have a nice selection to share with guests...with no extra effort!

Chocolate Lovers' Dream Cake

Carol Paffenroth
Pine Island, NY

A scrumptious cake for a special occasion...
garnish with a few ripe strawberries, if you like.

18-1/2 oz. pkg. super-moist
    butter recipe chocolate
    cake mix
1/2 c. chocolate milk
1/3 c. butter, melted
3 eggs, beaten

16-oz. container sour cream
3.4-oz. pkg. instant chocolate
    pudding mix
12-oz. pkg. semi-sweet
    chocolate chips

Mix together cake mix, milk, butter, eggs, sour cream and pudding
mix in a large bowl until well blended. Stir in chocolate chips; spoon
into a greased 12-cup Bundt® pan. Bake at 350 degrees for 55 to
60 minutes, until top springs back when touched. Cool in pan for
10 minutes; turn onto a serving plate and cool completely for 2 hours.
Drizzle Rich Chocolate Glaze over top. Makes 12 servings.

Rich Chocolate Glaze:

3/4 c. semi-sweet
    chocolate chips
3 T. butter

3 T. light corn syrup
1-1/2 t. water

Combine all ingredients in a small saucepan over low heat,
stirring frequently, until smooth.

Clip branches of bright red pepperberries to arrange in vases... they're
so pretty in autumn and will still be beautiful at Christmas time.

White Almond Fudge

Linda Nichols
Wintersville, OH

You'll love this candy...it tastes like you worked for hours!

10-oz. pkg. white chocolate
   chips
2/3 c. sweetened condensed
   milk

1-1/2 c. slivered almonds,
   toasted
1/2 t. vanilla extract

Combine chocolate chips and condensed milk in a saucepan over low heat; stir constantly until chocolate is melted. Remove from heat; stir in almonds and vanilla. Pour mixture into an aluminum foil-lined, greased 8"x8" baking pan. Cover and chill for several hours, until firm. Lift fudge from pan with foil. Peel off foil; cut into squares. Store in a cool, dry place. Makes about 2 dozen pieces.

Choco-Raisin Fudge

Ruth Miller
North Apollo, PA

Tastes like your favorite chunky candy bar, but better!

12-oz. pkg. semi-sweet
   chocolate chips
1 c. crunchy peanut butter

3 c. mini marshmallows
3/4 c. raisins

Melt chocolate chips and peanut butter in a saucepan over low heat. Fold in marshmallows and raisins; stir until marshmallows are melted. Pour into a greased 11"x7" baking pan; chill until firm. Cut into squares. Store in a cool, dry place. Makes 2 to 3 dozen pieces.

Making fudge is cozy family fun. Give everyone
their own spoon to lick the pan afterwards...yum!

Oatmeal Carmelitas

Joyce LaMure
Reno, NV

*Greet the kids with an after-school treat...glasses of
ice-cold milk and a plate of these chewy bar cookies.*

1 c. plus 3 T. all-purpose flour,
   divided
1 c. quick-cooking oats,
   uncooked
3/4 c. brown sugar, packed
1/2 t. baking soda

1/4 t. salt
3/4 c. butter, melted
1 c. semi-sweet chocolate chips
1/2 c. chopped pecans
3/4 c. caramel ice cream topping

Combine one cup flour, oats, brown sugar, baking soda, salt and
melted butter. Blend with an electric mixer on low speed to form a
crumbly mixture. Press half into an ungreased 11"x7" baking pan;
bake at 350 degrees for 10 minutes. Remove from oven. Sprinkle
with chocolate chips and pecans; set aside. Combine topping and
remaining flour; drizzle over top. Sprinkle with remaining crumb
mixture. Bake for an additional 15 to 20 minutes, until golden.
Chill for one to 2 hours; cut into bars. Makes about 2 dozen.

Be sure to pick up a pint or 2 of ice cream in pumpkin,
cinnamon and other delicious seasonal flavors when they're
available...they add that special touch to holiday meals!

S'mores Pudding Pie

Dana Thompson
Gooseberry Patch

Our favorite campfire flavors in a slice of pie.

7-oz. jar marshmallow creme
9-inch graham cracker crust
3.9-oz. pkg. instant chocolate
    pudding mix

1 c. hard-shell chocolate topping
Optional: whipped topping,
    mini chocolate chips

Spread marshmallow creme gently in crust and set aside. Prepare pudding mix according to package instructions; pour pudding over marshmallow creme. Spread topping over pie. Chill for 1-1/2 hours. If desired, garnish with dollops of whipped topping and a sprinkle of mini chocolate chips. Makes 8 servings.

Stir up some old-fashioned fun this Halloween. Light the house with spooky candlelight and serve homemade popcorn balls, pumpkin cookies and hot cider. Bob for apples and play pin the tail on the black cat...kids from 6 to 76 will love it!

Old-Time Popcorn Balls

Jill Valentine
Jackson, TN

Wrap in orange cellophane and heap in a wooden bowl
for your next Halloween party...guests will love 'em!

16 c. popped popcorn
2 c. molasses
1 c. sugar

2 T. butter
1/2 t. salt
1 t. baking soda

Place popped corn in a roaster pan; set aside. Combine molasses, sugar, butter and salt in a heavy saucepan over medium-high heat. Boil, stirring occasionally, until mixture reaches the hard-ball stage, or 250 to 269 degrees on a candy thermometer. Remove from heat; add baking soda and mix well. Pour over popped corn; stir to coat each kernel well. With well-buttered hands, quickly shape into balls. Makes one to 1-1/2 dozen balls.

No-Fuss Caramel Corn

Crystal Myers
Hillsboro, OH

So much tastier than store-bought caramel corn!

12 c. popped popcorn
Optional: 1-1/2 c. peanuts
1 c. brown sugar, packed
1/2 c. butter

1/4 c. light corn syrup
1/2 t. salt
1/2 t. baking soda

Place popcorn in a large brown paper bag; add peanuts, if using, and set aside. Combine brown sugar, butter, corn syrup and salt in a microwave-safe 2-quart glass bowl. Microwave on high setting for 3 to 4 minutes, stirring after each minute, until mixture comes to a boil. Microwave for 2 additional minutes without stirring. Stir in baking soda. Pour mixture over popcorn; close bag and shake well. Microwave in bag for 1-1/2 minutes. Shake bag well and pour into a roaster pan; cool and stir. Makes about 12 cups.

Cinnamon Poached Pears

Melanie Lowe
Dover, DE

*A light dessert that's not too sweet, or serve as
a delicious side dish for roast chicken.*

4 pears
1 c. pear nectar
1 c. water
3/4 c. maple syrup

2 4-inch cinnamon sticks,
   slightly crushed
4 strips lemon zest

Peel and core pears from the bottom, leaving stems intact. Cut a thin slice off bottom so pears will stand up; set aside. Combine remaining ingredients in a Dutch oven. Bring to a boil over medium heat, stirring occasionally. Add pears, standing right-side up. Reduce heat and simmer, covered, for 20 to 30 minutes, until tender. Remove pears from saucepan. Continue to simmer sauce in pan until reduced to 3/4 cup, about 15 minutes. Serve pears drizzled with sauce. Serves 4.

Fill a big apothecary jar with penny candy sticks in orange,
lemon yellow, golden butterscotch, chocolate brown and
other autumn colors. So pretty on a sideboard...
invite each guest to choose a favorite!

Festive Cranberry Cobbler

Dawn Psik
Aliquippa, PA

The main ingredients can be kept on hand in the cupboard,
ready to whip up a warm, cozy dessert for the family anytime.

18-1/2 oz. pkg. yellow cake mix
1/2 t. cinnamon
1/4 t. nutmeg
1 c. butter, softened
1/2 c. chopped pecans

21-oz. can peach pie filling
16-oz. can whole-berry
    cranberry sauce
Garnish: vanilla ice cream

Combine cake mix and spices in a large bowl; cut in butter with a pastry cutter until crumbly. Stir in pecans; set aside. Combine pie filling and cranberry sauce in an ungreased 13"x9" baking pan; mix well. Sprinkle crumb mixture over fruit. Bake at 350 degrees for 45 to 50 minutes, until golden. Serve warm with ice cream. Serves 6 to 8.

Pick up some mini wooden birdhouses from a craft store to paint as haunted houses. Line them up along a mantel or group them together as an amusing centerpiece...oh-so clever!

Pumpkin Gingerbread Cake

Glenna Tooman
Boise, ID

Every time I serve this for dessert, I get requests for the recipe!

3 c. sugar
1 c. oil
4 eggs
2/3 c. water
15-oz. can pumpkin
2 t. ground ginger
1 t. cinnamon
1 t. allspice

1 t. nutmeg
1 t. ground cloves
3-1/2 c. all-purpose flour
2 t. baking soda
1/2 t. baking powder
1-1/2 t. salt
Garnish: 8-oz. container frozen
    whipped topping, thawed

Beat together sugar, oil and eggs. Add water; mix well. Beat in pumpkin and spices; set aside. In a separate bowl, combine flour, baking soda, baking powder and salt. Stir into pumpkin mixture just until dry ingredients are moistened. Pour into a greased 13"x9" baking pan; bake at 350 degrees for about 45 minutes, until a toothpick tests clean. Cool slightly. Serve warm or cold, garnished with whipped topping. Serves 12.

Arrange wedges of crisp apples around a bowl of
caramel ice cream topping so guests can dip away...yum!

Caramel Apple Dessert

Lee Ann Stamper
Temecula, CA

Set the punch bowl in a wreath of fall mums...perfect for a party!

18-1/4 oz. pkg. yellow cake mix
6 c. milk
3 3.4-oz. pkgs. instant vanilla
   pudding mix
1 t. apple pie spice
12-1/4 oz. jar caramel
   ice cream topping, divided

1-1/2 c. chopped pecans, toasted
   and divided
2 21-oz. cans apple pie filling
2 16-oz. containers frozen
   whipped topping, thawed

Bake cake according to package directions, using 2 greased 9" round cake pans. In a large bowl, beat together milk, pudding mix and spice with an electric mixer on medium speed for 2 minutes; set aside. Cut one cake layer to fit evenly in an 8-quart punch bowl. Poke holes in cake with a skewer; pour 1/3 of caramel topping over cake, sprinkle with 1/2 cup pecans and spread half of pudding mixture over top. Spoon one can pie filling over pudding mixture; spread one container whipped topping over top. Top with remaining cake layer; repeat layers. Drizzle with remaining caramel; sprinkle with remaining pecans. Refrigerate until ready to serve. Makes 15 to 20 servings.

A surprising fact...sweet-scented beeswax candles
will last longer if they're stored in the freezer.

Swedish Ginger Cookies

Lisa Ashton
Aston, PA

The orange zest really brings out the flavor of the ginger.

1 c. margarine, softened
1-1/2 c. sugar
1 egg, beaten
2 T. dark corn syrup
1 T. water
1-1/2 T. orange zest

3-1/4 c. all-purpose flour
2 t. baking soda
2 t. cinnamon
1 t. ground ginger
Garnish: sugar

Beat together margarine and sugar in a large bowl; add egg and beat until light and fluffy. Add corn syrup, water and zest; set aside. Sift together flour, baking soda and spices; gradually add to margarine mixture. Roll dough into walnut-size balls; place on ungreased baking sheets. Press a fork dipped in sugar onto cookies to flatten. Bake at 375 degrees for 8 to 10 minutes. Makes about 8 dozen.

A tasty treat for classroom parties...top
chocolate-frosted cupcakes with candy pumpkins and a
sprinkle of green-tinted coconut "grass." Kids will love 'em!

Molasses Oat Cookies

*Sherry Morefield Gregg
Bailey, CO*

*My girlfriend's mother, Jane Dohrmann, used to bake these cookies...
even as a young schoolchild I knew this recipe was a goodie!*

1/2 c. shortening
2 eggs
1-1/4 c. sugar
1/2 c. molasses
1-3/4 c. all-purpose flour
1 t. baking soda

1 t. salt
2 t. cinnamon
2 c. quick-cooking oats,
  uncooked
1 c. golden raisins
Optional: 1/2 c. chopped nuts

Combine shortening, eggs, sugar and molasses in a medium bowl;
mix thoroughly. Stir in flour, baking soda, salt and cinnamon.
Add oats, raisins and nuts, if using; mix well. Drop by teaspoonfuls
onto lightly greased baking sheets. Bake at 400 degrees for 8 to
10 minutes. Makes 3 to 4 dozen.

Gather 2 or 3 of your best girlfriends for an autumn tea party.
Over cookies and a pot of spiced tea, you can get caught
up on each other's summer vacations before the busy
Thanksgiving-to-Christmas season arrives.

Perfect Pumpkin Pie

Lois Bivens
Gooseberry Patch

*My mother revised this from an old label recipe to make
enough filling for 2 pies. It turns out creamy,
custardy and just spicy enough.*

29-oz. can pumpkin
1 c. sugar
1-1/4 t. salt
1-1/2 t. cinnamon
3/4 t. ground ginger
1/2 t. nutmeg

4 eggs, beaten
1-1/2 c. milk
1-1/2 c. evaporated milk
1/4 c. butter, melted
2 9-inch pie crusts
1 egg white, beaten

Combine pumpkin, sugar, salt and spices. Add eggs, milks
and butter; mix well and set aside. Place pie crusts in pie plates.
Brush crusts with egg white; divide pumpkin mixture evenly between
crusts. Bake at 450 degrees for 10 minutes. Reduce oven
to 350 degrees; bake for an additional 30 minutes, or until pumpkin
filling is firm. Makes 2 pies; each serves 6 to 8.

Roll out extra pie crust dough, cut with leaf-shaped mini cookie
cutters and press onto the top crust before baking. Or bake on
a baking sheet at 350 degrees until golden...a fun topper for
any kind of creamy pie.

Jennifer's Red-Ribbon Apple Pie

Jennifer Niemi
Meadowvale, Nova Scotia

This pie took first place at an exhibition…
first-place ribbons here in Canada are red, not blue!

1/4 c. all-purpose flour
2/3 c. plus 1 t. sugar, divided
1-1/2 t. cinnamon
1/2 t. nutmeg
1/2 t. allspice

1/8 t. salt
6 c. Granny Smith apples, cored,
   peeled and diced
1 T. lemon juice
2 9-inch pie crusts

Combine flour, 2/3 cup sugar, spices and salt in a small bowl; set aside. Toss together apples and lemon juice in a large bowl; stir in flour mixture, mixing well. Place one crust in a 9" pie plate; spoon filling into crust. Top with second crust and crimp edges; cut slits in top to vent. Bake at 425 degrees for 15 minutes; reduce oven to 350 degrees and bake for an additional 30 minutes. Remove from oven; immediately sprinkle with remaining sugar. Serves 8.

Who can dream of a Thanksgiving dinner without a pie!

-Fannie Farmer

Cranberry-Pecan Bars

Leslie Naugle
Columbia, MO

Cut these yummy bar cookies into smaller squares and place in frilly paper muffin liners for a just-a-bite addition to a sweets tray.

1 c. plus 2 T. all-purpose flour, divided
1-1/4 c. plus 2 T. sugar, divided
1/3 c. butter
1 c. pecans, finely chopped and divided

2 eggs, beaten
2 T. milk
1 T. orange zest
1 t. vanilla extract
1 c. cranberries, chopped
1/2 c. sweetened flaked coconut

Combine one cup flour and 2 tablespoons sugar in a medium bowl; cut in butter with a pastry cutter until mixture resembles coarse crumbs. Stir in half the pecans; press mixture into an ungreased 13"x9" baking pan. Bake at 350 degrees for 15 minutes; set aside. Combine remaining sugar and flour. Stir in eggs, milk, zest and vanilla; fold in cranberries, coconut and remaining pecans. Spread over crust; bake for an additional 25 to 30 minutes, or until golden. Cut into bars while warm. Makes about 3 dozen.

Stock up on fresh cranberries when they're available every autumn to add their fruity tang to cookies, quick breads and sauces year 'round. Simply pop unopened bags in the freezer.

Seasonal
SWEETS

Apple Butterscotch Bars

Karen Hughes
Lewis Center, OH

These are really yummy!

2 c. sugar
1 c. oil
3 eggs, beaten
1 t. vanilla extract
2-1/2 c. all-purpose flour
2 t. baking powder
1 t. baking soda

1 t. salt
1 t. cinnamon
3 c. apples, cored, peeled
    and chopped
1 c. chopped nuts
1 c. butterscotch chips

Combine sugar, oil, eggs and vanilla in a large bowl. Mix in flour, baking powder, baking soda, salt and cinnamon; mix well. Stir in apples and nuts. Spread in a lightly greased 13"x9" baking pan. Bake at 350 degrees for 40 to 45 minutes. Makes about 3 dozen.

With guests sure to visit for the holidays, create an inviting
cottage-style guest room. A few little touches like a patchwork
quilt on the bed, a rocking chair and a cozy throw all say,
"We're glad you're here!"

Sweet Potato Cake

Sharon Tillman
Hampton, VA

*For an extra-special cake, bake 4 thin layers and assemble
with frosting...sprinkle crystallized ginger over the top.*

2-1/4 c. cake flour
1 T. baking powder
1/2 t. baking soda
1/2 t. salt
1-1/2 t. cinnamon
1/2 t. allspice
1/2 t. ground ginger
3/4 c. buttermilk

3/4 c. mashed sweet potatoes
1/2 c. golden raisins
1/2 c. butter
2 eggs
1 c. brown sugar, packed
1 c. sugar
16-oz. container buttercream
    frosting

Mix together flour, baking powder, baking soda, salt and spices in
a medium bowl; set aside. Mix together buttermilk, sweet potatoes
and raisins in a small bowl; set aside. In a large bowl, beat butter until
light and fluffy; add eggs one at a time, mixing thoroughly after each.
Gradually add brown sugar and sugar, beating until fluffy. Add flour
mixture alternately with buttermilk mixture, stirring just until smooth
after each addition. Pour batter into two, greased 9" round cake pans.
Bake at 350 degrees for 30 minutes, or until cake tests done. Cool;
remove layers from pans and assemble with frosting. Serves 12.

Save orange peels from breakfast, cut into strips and let dry.
Drop a few strips into a saucepan of water along with some
whole cloves and cinnamon sticks. Bring to a low simmer...
the spicy scent will be delicious!

Topsy-Turvy Pear Cake

*Carol Lytle
Columbus, OH*

A delicious twist on Grandma's pineapple upside-down cake.

3 pears, cored, peeled and
   halved
1-1/2 c. all-purpose flour
3/4 t. baking soda
1/2 t. salt
1 t. cinnamon
1/2 t. ground ginger
1/4 t. ground cloves

1/2 c. buttermilk
1/4 c. shortening
1/4 c. sugar
1 egg
1/2 c. molasses
1/4 c. chopped nuts
Garnish: whipped topping

Arrange pear halves in a greased 9" round cake pan, cut-side down and stem ends toward center; set aside. Combine flour, baking soda, salt and spices in a large bowl; set aside. Combine buttermilk, shortening, sugar, egg and molasses in a blender. Blend until smooth, about 2 minutes. Pour over flour mixture and mix thoroughly. Pour batter over pears; sprinkle with nuts. Bake at 350 degrees for 40 to 45 minutes. Immediately loosen cake from edges of pan and turn onto a serving plate. Serve warm with whipped topping. Serves 6.

Juicy fresh pears are one of fall's delights. Green Anjou pears and sandy-colored Bosc will hold their shape nicely when cooked, while red or yellow Bartlett pears are delicious for eating out of hand.

Grandma Lena's Bread Pudding

Carolyn Finkelmeier
Cincinnati, OH

This recipe has been in my family for at least 85 years.
It's the only bread pudding I've ever seen that has
meringue on top...and it is so, so good!

5 slices day-old white bread,
    cubed
2 c. milk
1/2 c. butter

1-1/4 c. sugar, divided
4 eggs, separated
1 t. vanilla extract
Garnish: maraschino cherries

Place bread cubes in a large bowl; set aside. Heat milk just to boiling and pour over bread. Blend butter, 3/4 cup sugar, egg yolks and vanilla together until smooth; stir into bread mixture. Pour into a greased 8"x8" baking pan. Bake at 350 degrees for 30 minutes, or until set. Beat egg whites until stiff with an electric mixer on high setting; add remaining sugar. Beat again; spread over baked pudding, sealing edges. Return to oven until golden, about 8 to 10 minutes. Cut into squares and top each with a cherry. Makes 9 servings.

For an easy harvest centerpiece, stack yellowware bowls
in pairs. Invert the larger bowl and set the smaller bowl
on top. Heap with apples or walnuts.

Toasted Pecan Pudding

Emma Wilson
Cordell, OK

This is best served the same day it's made.

1 c. chopped pecans
1/2 c. margarine, melted
1 c. all-purpose flour
1/4 c. brown sugar, packed
1-1/2 c. sweetened flaked
   coconut

2 3.4-oz. pkgs. instant vanilla
   pudding mix
3 c. milk
8-oz. container frozen whipped
   topping, thawed

Combine pecans, margarine, flour, brown sugar and coconut; spread
in an ungreased 15"x10" jelly-roll pan. Bake at 325 degrees for
30 minutes, or until golden, stirring occasionally; cool. In a large bowl,
beat together pudding mix and milk with an electric mixer on low
speed for 2 minutes. Chill for 5 minutes; fold in whipped topping.
Place half the pecan mixture in a lightly greased 13"x9" baking pan;
spread pudding mixture carefully over top. Top with remaining pecan
mixture; chill. Serves 10 to 12.

Toasting really brings out the flavor of shelled nuts...and it's
oh-so-easy! Place nuts in a small dry skillet. Cook and stir over
low heat for a few minutes until toasty and golden...that's all!

Apple Hand Pies

Rita Morgan
Pueblo, CO

Taste just like the fried pies at the county fair.

2 apples, cored, peeled and diced
1/3 c. sugar
1/2 t. cinnamon
2 c. all-purpose flour
1 t. salt

1/2 c. shortening
1/2 c. cold water
1 c. oil
Garnish: powdered sugar

Stir together apples, sugar and cinnamon in a saucepan. Cook over low heat for 8 to 10 minutes, until apples are tender. Set aside. Combine flour and salt; cut in shortening with a fork. Stir in water to a dough consistency. Roll out dough 1/8-inch thick on a floured surface. Cut out with a 4-inch round cookie cutter; place one tablespoon apple mixture in center of each circle. Sprinkle edges with water; fold circles in half. Seal edges with a fork; set aside. Heat oil in a skillet over medium-high heat. Fry pies, a few at a time, for 2 to 3 minutes on each side, until golden. Drain on paper towels; sprinkle with powdered sugar while still warm. Makes 6 to 8 pies.

Throw a pumpkin painting party! Provide acrylic paints, brushes and plenty of pumpkins...invite kids to bring their imagination and an old shirt to wear as a smock. Parents are sure to join in too!

Raisin Butter Tarts

Beth Kramer
Port Saint Lucie, FL

Sweet, dainty tarts, just right for a tea tray.

14 4-inch tart crusts
1 egg
1 c. brown sugar, packed
3 T. butter, melted

2 T. lemon juice
1/4 t. nutmeg
1 c. raisins
Garnish: whipped cream

Bake tart crusts as package directs; cool in pan. Beat together egg and brown sugar until well blended; stir in remaining ingredients except crusts. Fill crusts 1/2 full. Bake at 375 degrees for 15 to 20 minutes. Cool tarts in pan for several minutes; remove to a wire rack to finish cooling. Top with whipped cream. Makes 14 tarts.

Friendship Spiced Tea Mix

Lavenna Carey
Springfield, OH

My sister-in-law and I would get together in the evenings to do our craft painting. She always had a cup of this hot tea ready for me when I came through her door. It gave me such a warm cozy feeling!

6-oz. container lemonade
   drink mix
2 c. orange-flavored drink mix

1-1/2 c. instant tea
1/2 c. sugar
2 t. ground cloves

Mix all ingredients well; store in an airtight container. To serve, place one cup of boiling water in a mug; stir in 4 teaspoons of tea mix. Makes 19 servings.

Pumpkin Ice Cream Pie

Beth Cavanaugh
Gooseberry Patch

You'll harvest compliments on this cool, creamy dessert.

15-oz. can pumpkin
1/4 c. sugar
1-1/2 t. pumpkin pie spice

1 qt. vanilla ice cream, softened
9-inch graham cracker crust
Optional: whipped topping

Mix together pumpkin, sugar and spice until well blended. Quickly fold into ice cream. Pour into crust and freeze, uncovered, until firm, about 2 hours. Cover with plastic wrap and aluminum foil; return to freezer until ready to serve. Thaw pie slightly before serving. Garnish with whipped topping, if desired. Serves 8.

String dried apple slices, cinnamon sticks and star anise
on sturdy thread to make swags for the kitchen.

Candy Apple Cheesecake

Sherry Gordon
Arlington Heights, IL

Scrumptious any time of year.

21-oz. can apple pie filling,
    divided
9-inch graham cracker crust
2 8-oz. pkgs. cream cheese,
    softened
1/2 c. sugar

1/2 t. vanilla extract
2 eggs
1/2 c. caramel ice cream topping
12 pecan halves
2 T. chopped pecans

Reserve 1/2 cup apple pie filling; spoon remaining filling into crust.
Beat together cream cheese, sugar and vanilla extract until smooth.
Add eggs and beat well; pour over filling. Bake at 350 degrees for
35 minutes, or until center is set; cool. Mix reserved apple filling and
caramel topping in a small saucepan; heat for about one minute.
Spoon caramel mixture evenly onto cheesecake. Arrange pecan halves
around edge; sprinkle with chopped pecans. Keep chilled until serving
time. Serves 8 to 12.

Teacup candles...fill delicate flowered vintage teacups
with scented wax crystals and slip in a wick. It's nice
to have a few on hand for gifts to special visitors!

Autumn Fruit Crisp

Eleanor Paternoster
Bridgeport, CT

An old-fashioned delight.

6 c. Golden Delicious apples,
  cored, peeled and sliced
1 c. sweetened, dried cherries
1/2 c. sugar
1 T. orange zest
3 t. cinnamon, divided
1 c. all-purpose flour

1 c. quick-cooking oats,
  uncooked
3/4 c. brown sugar, packed
1 t. ground ginger
1/4 t. mace
3/4 c. butter, softened
Garnish: ice cream

In a large bowl, combine apples, cherries, sugar, zest and one teaspoon cinnamon. Toss well and place in a slow cooker that has been sprayed with non-stick vegetable spray; set aside. In another bowl, mix flour, oats, brown sugar, ginger, mace and remaining cinnamon; stir to combine. Crumble butter with your fingers; add to flour mixture and knead to mix. Sprinkle over fruit mixture, patting down lightly. Cover and cook on high setting for 4 hours, until hot and bubbly. Serve warm with ice cream. Makes 12 servings.

Scoops of ice cream are a perfect garnish for warm autumn pies and puddings. Serve them in a snap...simply scoop ahead of time into paper muffin liners and freeze on a baking sheet.

Golden Raisin Bread Pudding

Maryellen Meden
Arlington, VA

Real comfort food...delicious any time of day!

4 c. white bread, toasted and
    cubed
3/4 c. golden raisins
2 eggs
3/4 c. sugar
2-1/2 c. milk, heated to boiling
    and cooled

2 T. butter, melted
1 t. vanilla extract
1/2 t. cinnamon
1/8 t. nutmeg
1/8 t. salt
Garnish: whipped cream

Combine bread cubes and raisins in a slow cooker that has been sprayed with non-stick vegetable spray; set aside. In a medium bowl, beat eggs and sugar; whisk in cooled milk, butter, vanilla, spices and salt. Pour over bread, pressing down so bread will soak up milk mixture. Cover and cook on low setting for 6 hours. Serve warm, topped with whipped cream. Makes 8 servings.

Tuck odds & ends of leftover sliced bread, croissants and even cinnamon rolls into a freezer container. Before long, you'll have enough for a yummy bread pudding!

INDEX

INDEX

INDEX

We've cooked up a whole collection of Gooseberry Patch® books!

Have a taste for more? Call us toll-free at
1-800-854-6673
We'll send you our latest catalog filled with kitchenware, candles, handmade quilts, gourmet goodies, enamelware, bowls, night lights and our very own line of cookbooks, calendars and organizers!

Phone us:
1·800·854·6673

Fax us:
1·740·363·7225

Visit our website:
www.gooseberrypatch.com

Send us your favorite recipe!

and the memory that makes it special for you! If we select your recipe for a brand-new **Gooseberry Patch** cookbook, your name will appear right along with it...and you'll receive a FREE copy of the book! Mail to:

Gooseberry Patch
Attn: Book Dept.
P.O. Box 190
Delaware, OH 43015

*Please include the number of servings and all other necessary information!

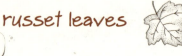 russet leaves warm spiced cider

spicy pumpkin pie

a country bonfire

harvest home

shine on, harvest moon

 suɹǝʇuɐๅ-,O-ʞɔɐſ 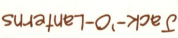 pumpkin patch

U.S. to Canadian recipe equivalents

Volume Measurements

1/4 teaspoon	1 mL
1/2 teaspoon	2 mL
1 teaspoon	5 mL
1 tablespoon = 3 teaspoons	15 mL
2 tablespoons = 1 fluid ounce	30 mL
1/4 cup	60 mL
1/3 cup	75 mL
1/2 cup = 4 fluid ounces	125 mL
1 cup = 8 fluid ounces	250 mL
2 cups = 1 pint =16 fluid ounces	500 mL
4 cups = 1 quart	1 L

Weights

1 ounce	30 g
4 ounces	120 g
8 ounces	225 g
16 ounces = 1 pound	450 g

Oven Temperatures

300° F	150° C
325° F	160° C
350° F	180° C
375° F	190° C
400° F	200° C
450° F	230° C

Baking Pan Sizes

Square

8x8x2 inches	2 L = 20x20x5 cm
9x9x2 inches	2.5 L = 23x23x5 cm

Rectangular

13x9x2 inches	3.5 L = 33x23x5 cm

Loaf

9x5x3 inches	2 L = 23x13x7 cm

Round

8x1-1/2 inches	1.2 L = 20x4 cm
9x1-1/2 inches	1.5 L = 23x4 cm